Anne Martindell

NEVER TOO LATE

A Memoir

Boxed Books, Inc. Lawrenceville, NJ

NEVER TOO LATE

International Standard Book Number:
978-1933672502

Dedicated to my Children

Library of Congress Control Number: 2008924272

Printed in the United States of America

First Edition

10 9 8 7 6 5 4 3 2 1

Boxed Books titles are available at special discounts for bulk purchases by corporations, institutions, and other organizations. For more information, please contact the Publisher, Boxed Books, Inc., 19 Woodlane Road, Lawrenceville, NJ 08648

Acknowledgements

So many people helped me with the writing of this book. I am grateful for the support from so many, especially my children, Marjory, George, David, and Roger. In addition I was inspired, supported and encouraged by Madeline Albright, Wendy Benchley, Blanche Brann, Carol Moseley Braun, Marilyn Brice, Brendan Byrne, Mary Bundy, Jimmy and Roslynn Carter, Hodding Carter, Ethel Chipowski, Carol Christ, Joanna Clark, Timothy and Hannah Clark, Paul and Joan Cleveland, Kate and Robert Del Tufo, Patt Derian, Bob and Margaret Goheen, Robert and Marjo Graff, Rachel Gray, Samuel Hamill, Bill and Leita Hamill, Russell Hemingway, Janet and James Hester, Richard Holbrooke, Christian Holmes, Rush Holt, Daniel Horowitz, Nicholas and Lydia Katzenbach, Annalise Kennan, Margaret Lancefield, Ryan Lilienthal, Ruth Mandel, Russell and Patricia Marks, Elsbeth Savage McClennan, John McGoldrick, Juliana McIntyre, Sam and Eileen Moffett, Nancy Muir, Paul Muldoon, Philip Norkelinus, Malcolm Ott, Ruth Perkins, Meredith Prime, William and Joan Roth, Ellie Rothman, Victor Schaffner, Ruth Simmons, Ian Frazier and Susan Snively, Gloria Steinem, John and Judy Thompson, Richard and Gail Ullman, Ann Waldron, Debbie Walsh, Captain Westbrook, Sean Wilentz, Susan and Don Wilson, Frank Wisner, Phillip Woollaston, and Toss Woollaston.

Dedication

To my children

Marjory, David, George and Roger,
and to my friend Lydia Katzenbach,
who suggested this book be written.

Prologue

On a bright September day in 1999, my granddaughter Katie and I drove up Interstate 91 to Northampton, Massachusetts, in my blue Audi. In the trunk were several suitcases and boxes I had packed carefully. I was on my way to enroll for the second time as an undergraduate at Smith College. The first time was in 1932 when my mother, and my roommate, Mary Rogers, accompanied me in our chauffeur–driven maroon custom Lincoln. My trunks, packed by Mimi, the French maid, had been sent ahead by train. This time I intended to complete the education I had started 67 years earlier. My plan would be to graduate in three years, in 2002. No one would stop me this time.

In 1932 my feelings and expectations ran high, excited at the thought of being on my own at last, at a "grown–up" institution, away from home and the atmosphere of tension and anger that existed between my parents. But at the same time, I was nervous about this new venture. In her inimitable fashion, my mother instructed my roommate and me to budget our time efficiently—urging us to organize, to get up early, tidy our rooms, and get to our classes on time. She provided canvas–covered boxes in which to send dirty laundry home.

I told Katie about that first trip to Northampton and then about the events of the intervening years. First, marriage to the grandfather she never knew, then divorce and remarriage, four children, nine grandchildren, and six great–grandchildren. I described the sea change at midlife when I dived into a job teaching young children to read using

1

a new and innovative process. I had no specific training and yet discovering I could do it well gave me a measure of self–confidence.

I grew from being a shy, very conventional woman, one trained not to deviate from the financially secure but emotionally empty script that had been written for me, to being one ready to take chances. Initially, I had honed my skills as a fundraiser for schools; shortly thereafter, I moved into politics, first as a fundraiser, then into a Democratic Party position, then to election as a state senator, appointment as director of Foreign Disaster Assistance, and eventually to ambassador to New Zealand. In New Zealand I met Toss Woollaston, the country's leading painter, who became the love of my life.

My old friend and former schoolmate Kate asked me why I decided to return to Smith 52 years later. At this time of my life, a question I had heard in one form or another from many friends and colleagues. I told her that my decision came as a result of an intersection of things: I had loved my freshman year at Smith and had always longed to return, filling the gaps with other university courses at different periods of my life. Now, I sought to fill the emptiness created by Toss's death. Smith College had created the Ada Comstock Scholars Program that encouraged and supported older women who wished to complete their bachelor's degree at the college. The Program, founded in 1975 under able management of its director, Ellie Rothman, was established to support and assist women of nontraditional age to complete undergraduate education. Although admissions standards were high, comparable with those of traditional students, the program intentionally set neither age limits on enrollment nor time limits on the completion of a degree. Women who had other work or family responsibilities had the benefit of flexible schedules, though all graduates were required to complete two full years on campus.

Although a large number of Adas, as they were affectionately called, received financial assistance, I knew I wouldn't qualify for that. I would need to rent an apartment on campus and had to pay full tuition. It was an expensive proposition, but I knew that it was worth every dollar of the investment.

My granddaughter Katie had just graduated from law school in San Diego and expected to settle there. She had specialized in criminal law, hoping to become a public defender. She, as well as my children and other grandchildren, offered enthusiastic support for my new adventure. Something about their confidence, their unquestioning support made my return to Smith at the age of eighty–five seemed less unusual. It would be the fulfillment of a dream I had for over 50 years—to finally finish college after a life of many achievements.

We entered Northampton and drove slowly along Main Street. Up a short hill stood the wrought iron Grecourt Gates, their graceful arabesques framing College Hall, the building housing the President's Office and those of other administrators. Past the gates we could see the geometric green lawns and courtyards, which outlined other once familiar college buildings: the art museum, where I had spent many happy hours; John M. Greene Hall, a mahogany red auditorium with looming Greco–Roman pillars; Neilson Library, with its long wooden study tables and famed Rare Book Room I remembered. We turned into the center of the campus, passing Paradise Pond, a serene sheet of water on which I had rowed in the spring of 1933. Legend has it that when the noted Swedish soprano Jenny Lind visited Northampton in the nineteenth century, she walked beside the pond and exclaimed, "This must be paradise." Ever after, it was.

We were directed by a Smith official, meeting incoming students, to the "ITT Building" for registration.

"ITT, the telephone company?" I asked.

"Indoor Track and Tennis," said the official, "down past Paradise Pond."

In front of the ITT were long lines of entering students, most with parents, waiting to pick up their room–and–board contracts and keys. All I had to do was pick up my mailbox key and have my picture taken for my student ID card.

Katie and I walked across the lawn where tables were set up and soft drinks were being served. I looked around at the entering students: most wore blue jeans, a few ankle–length skirts, and some wore shorts. Here and there I could see bright pink, iridescent green, or metallic purple heads of hair. Some students had body piercing: noses, tongues, and lips. I smiled at the fleeting thought that my mother would have approved of my present costume: a blouse and a skirt, something very similar to what I wore in 1932.

How students dressed or how they expressed themselves were simply symptoms of much larger and deeper changes in Smith since my initial experiences there. A sexual revolution had swept the nation, and with it came many liberating consequences for women. I could hardly be surprised about the impact of changes in behavior and values spawned by that revolution that were clearly visible now at Smith. After all, Betty Friedan, whose book *The Feminine Mystique* many consider the bible of that revolution, and Gloria Steinem, whose popular magazine *Ms.* carried articles by America's foremost feminist thinkers, were both Smith graduates.

Challenges to patriarchal authority with its prescribed roles, the availability of reliable birth control, and a much keener sense of gender inequalities in the work place opened a whole new vista of possibilities for Smith undergraduates. Minority admissions rose, a much higher percentage of Smith students were admitted on scholarships, and a women's studies program was established. In short, not only did Smith look different, it was different. Smith had grown just as surely as I had; we were in a much better position to intersect.

Although I had not yet spotted any women who looked like they might be fellow Ada Comstock Scholars, I knew I would in due time. The Ada Comstock Scholars Program was a great success by the time I was considering returning to Smith. Charles Kuralt on the *CBS Sunday Morning* show had reported on the graduating Adas in 1985, 1986, and 1987. In one widely watched segment he described the May 1985, Ada Comstock graduates as "The Classiest Class of '85." By 1999, more than 300 well–qualified older women, proud to be Adas, circulated through Smith's classes earning the respect of teachers and traditional students alike. I was proud to be admitted as an Ada–the oldest to enroll, as a matter of fact–proud to have my age and life experience count as an advantage, not a liability.

All too soon it was time to take Katie to the train. I said my goodbye, kissed her, and returned to the task of organizing my apartment. The building where my apartment was located had been the town high school in 1932, so it contained two large windows almost from floor to ceiling in the bedroom and living room through which the morning sun poured. I bought blue and white striped sheets and turned them into curtains, framing the windows. My blue sofa bed served as both a bed and a reading corner. Near the door was a small but adequate kitchen and opposite it, the bathroom. My small garden table served for all dining. I had brought a painting and two watercolors of Toss's and many family photos to keep from being homesick. It didn't work. I missed everybody, but this was my new mission in life, one that would fulfill my interrupted dreams of 1933.

My friend Liz Land lived directly above me on the third

floor, and down the hall from her were two other Adas. The apartment to my left was occupied by the social secretary to Ruth Simmons, Smith's president. I had met Ruth earlier when she was assistant provost at Princeton University. In fact, I had been so impressed by her dignity and poise that I drove up to Smith to attend her installation. I fully expected that Ruth Simmons's presidency would be an exciting and innovative time at Smith. Indeed, it proved to be just that. Not only did she attract more superbly qualified minority students, she raised money for a multi–million dollar student center and a new program in engineering before leaving to assume the presidency of Brown University. I concluded that my living arrangements were going to be very satisfactory, even if they were very different from my dorm room in 1932.

The orientation meeting in Seelye Hall interrupted my unpacking. First we were introduced to the nutritionist, then the head of psychiatric services, and the college doctor, who assured us that "HIV tests were available."

We toured the Neilson Library, called "The Libe" in 1932 and the place where I spent long hours studying. After the tour, I went to the archives and read the entire *Smith College Weekly* from 1932 to 1933. The ads took me back to another time: woolen coats with seal fur collars, a dozen different kinds of cigarettes targeting especially women. But I also gleaned from reading the *Weekly* that far more political activity went on at Smith in 1932 than I had been aware of at the time. The paper was published in the depths of the Depression, and many articles made references to the Liberal Club and the Progressive Club.

Once classes began, my day at Smith began early, six or six thirty a.m. The *New York Times* was at my door, and I read it quickly while eating breakfast by the window. On Tuesday and Thursday, my first class was Dan Horowitz's American Studies, an appropriate choice since American

Studies was my chosen major. Dan was tall, with dark hair and eyes. He was a wonderfully animated teacher who had the habit of throwing out questions to the class to generate discussion. Rumor had it that he was the model for the professor in the TV series, *The Education of Max Bickford.* Richard Dreyfus played Professor Bickford. During one class, Dan announced that he was monogamous and intended to stay that way; I wondered if some students had hopes of seducing him based on what they had seen on TV.

After American Studies, I'd rush back to the apartment for a cup of soup before the Art History class "Valesquez Backward and Forward." Toss had admired Valesquez and had painted a version of the famous "Las Meninas." The course was taught by Professor Felton in the Hillier Building, right next to the Art Museum. Although the Museum was more modern than I remembered, it retained its capacity to move me deeply.

On the days I did not have classes, I'd do the required reading and think about assigned papers. Sometimes, in order to break the routine, Liz Land and I would treat ourselves to lunch at the Faculty Club or the Green Street Café, a small bistro across the street from the campus. My study spaces were considerably more comfortable than they were in 1932 when we studied in the library at one of the large tables under rather dim lights. I remember my roommate, who never studied late, turned out the light at ten, chasing me across the hall to the bathroom. There I studied in the empty tub, one bulb hanging from the ceiling to barely light the pages. It must have paid off, because I made the honor roll that first year.

In 1999, one thing had not changed. I still wrote my papers in long hand. My computer skills were marginal, too slow for efficient typing. It seemed sensible to put a notice up on the bulletin board asking for assistance with the computer. Several students replied. Ruthemma, a fellow sophomore— though somewhat younger—was helpful and lots of fun to work with. She'd come for supper, sometimes with her roommate, and then we'd work on the paper at hand. Ruthemma, the daughter of a friend of my daughter Marjory, was also from Ann Arbor, Michigan. She was vivacious, petite, with blonde hair and blue eyes. She regaled me with stories about the "student life of trads" (traditional students). One tale involved Umass men who thought Smith women were so starved for sex that when invited to come to an event, they assumed they'd be asked to "sleep over."

Fall gave way to winter; December arrived, books were read, papers handed in, and I packed up to leave at the end of the semester. The additional required semester on the Smith College Campus would be scheduled next fall. During the spring term, I would take a course at Princeton University and do an Independent Study for Smith. Dan Horowitz, now my advisor, had worked out my curriculum for the two years, and it had been approved. I was scheduled to graduate in 2002—69 years after I first enrolled. This gave new definition to the term "late bloomer."

Fall Semester 1999 marked my second incarnation at Smith. As I lived within its familiar echoes and startling differences, I began to examine those forces that had brought me to the Grecourt Gates 67 years earlier. I discovered that it was quite a story, and so I began to write this memoir.

The usual reason for writing a memoir is to make a record for your children, grandchildren and friends, and to try to gain a perspective on your life. My goal is to inspire all of us to live fuller lives; to accept that your life does not have to follow a linear path. You can start something new, accept new challenges, say "YES" instead of "NO." It's never too late to begin, to open up a new part of your life.

My most extraordinary experiences, with the exception

of my children, started later in life, at an age when many contemplate retirement. My dear friend Lydia Katzenbach wonders if I've lived my life out of order. I married and had children in my twenties, that's fairly typical. But I started my first career as an innkeeper in my thirties, my second career as a teacher in my forties and my third career as a politician in my fifties. I fell truly in love for the first time in my life in my sixties and received my college degree in my eighties. And now that I'm in my nineties, I still look forward to what's coming next.

I've tried to make sense of my life and to candidly reflect on my insecurities and disappointments while hopefully imparting my gratitude for all that was given me and to all those who believed in me.

My son Roger said something the other day when asked why he was running again for council in Princeton. He said that he had learned the value of public service from his mother. I beamed with pride. So I hope this story inspires others to go out, give back, and embrace something new. It's never too late. Carpe Diem.

Chapter One

Every afternoon when I was little, I went to visit Mummy. Nanny, in her starched white uniform, would take me from the nursery down along the corridor of our New York City apartment to the library. Nanny would knock on the door. A low, musical voice would answer: "Come in."

Nanny opened the door. I would see Mummy stretched out on the big maroon, velvet sofa in the library. She was dressed in a rose–colored tea gown, her dark hair pinned to the top of her head, ropes of pearls around her neck, with pearl earrings dangling from her ears. A bowl of roses stood on the table beside her.

This regular appointment was after Mummy got up from her afternoon nap, when she was liberated from her corset. In her view, in was unthinkable, if not immoral, to leave the house without wearing a corset. In the late afternoon, she always put on a dress called a tea gown, in a color that went perfectly with her mournful dark eyes and brown hair. She had an assortment of tea gowns in luminous shades of blue, green, red or violet, made of silk, velvet, and sometimes brocaded with threads of silver or gold.

"Don't you look pretty, dear." Mummy would nod in approval of my white frilly dress, the blue satin bow in my auburn hair, and the coral beads around my neck. Nanny made sure I was presentable.

"You look beautiful, Mummy," I would say shyly.

Mummy bent down to give me a cool kiss on my cheek. She always smelled delicious, like a bed of lilies of the valley.

"Has Anne been a good girl, Mary?" she would ask

11

Nanny.

Nanny's answer would always be the same: "Oh, yes, ma'am, she's a little angel."

"Then you may have a cookie, Anne." She would hand me a macaroon from a small china plate. Then she would dismiss Nanny. "You may go back to the boys, Mary." After Nanny left I shuddered from the chill in the air.

I would sit down on my little chair and look around the room. The soft green walls were lined with shelves and shelves of books that reached all the way to the ceiling. The carpet was a deep rose; the green and rose curtains would be already drawn against the night. My mother would read me Peter Rabbit. She read with affection for the stories she selected. I would watch the reflection of the fire on the silver tea service on the low table before the sofa while she read.

When our half–hour was up, Mummy would ring the bell for Nanny, who would bustle in.

"Thank you, Mummy," I would say. "Good night."

"Good night, Anne." Another cool kiss followed and Mummy would go back to reading her own book.

Nanny would take me back to the nursery where Agnes, Nanny's assistant, was helping my brother Willie to get ready for bed while Nanny gave my youngest brother, Blair, his bottle. Later she would take the pins out of her hair, and it would swing free and cascade down her back in black waves. When she would let me brush it for her, I felt important, like a grown–up.

Once we were all ready for bed, I'd get tucked in and hugged and kissed by Nanny. Then she would tell me a story. Nanny, a natural storyteller, was a young Irish woman Mummy had engaged soon after I was born. She knew all sorts of stories, mostly about the baby Jesus and his mother Mary.

"Your name is Mary, isn't it, Nanny? Just like the baby Jesus' mother?" I asked.

"Mary it is, and I'll be tucking you into bed. Hop in. Matthew, Mark, Luke and John, bless this bed that you lie on," she would say.

Feeling warm and loved, I would drift off to sleep. In my mind's eye, I could see Mummy alone in the library with a book open on her lap with no one to admire her tea gown, her gleaming pearls, her soft dark hair and sad, dark eyes, so often near tears.

As children, my brothers and I spent most of our time with nurses and governesses. Our mother was often ill; Father was usually away. First, he served in World War I; then he joined a big law firm—which meant long hours, long assignments, even months away in Chicago on a big case. We spent winters in the apartment at 125 East 72nd Street, not far from the grand house on 70th Street where Mummy's parents, Grandpa and Granny Blair, lived, and the one on East 68th Street where my Clark grandparents, Father's family resided. Summers we lived at the Post House, our house in Bernardsville, New Jersey, only a mile away from our Clark grandparents. Several miles farther away was Blairsden, the magnificent Blair summer residence, modeled after a French château.

Life was very comfortable. Grandpa Clark was President of the Clark Thread Company with mills in Newark that boasted a smokestack famous for being one of the tallest structures in the world at that time. Grandpa Blair was a descendent of and heir to John I. Blair, who had made his fortune in the railroad industry in the 19th century.

The Clark side of our family tree was sprinkled with memorable and accomplished persons. The British art critic, Kenneth Clark, was a cousin. My great–grandfather, Granny Clark's grandfather, Simon Cameron, was for a time Abraham Lincoln's Secretary of War and later became the Ambassador to Russia. Granny loved to tell the story of President Lincoln

and the Gettysburg Address. Simon Cameron, as former
senator from Pennsylvania, accompanied Lincoln on the train
as he traveled from Washington to Gettysburg. The President,
wanting to work on his speech, asked for a piece of paper. "My
grandfather took an envelope from his pocket and handed it
to the President," Granny would relate. "A late draft of that
speech was written on his envelope." Granny was a flinty
and upright Scotswoman, so I believed her story. At least I
believed she believed it.

Mummy was truly in love with Father when she married
him in 1913—and she loved him until the end of her life,
in spite of everything that was to come. However, she felt
intellectually inferior to his family. She had been brought up
and educated in the traditional fashion for women of her time,
taught first by a governess at home and then spent three years
at a fashionable boarding school and a year at a finishing
school in Paris. Father, who grew up in a family where books
and current affairs were the usual dinner table conversation,
was a formidable intellect and would eventually cap his legal
career with an appointment to the Third Circuit Court of
Appeals.

So Mummy read, every day and into the night in order
to catch up on the education she lacked and to earn her
husband's respect. And with at least eight servants, including
Nanny, Nanny's assistant Agnes, and Mimi, the French lady's
maid, she had plenty of time to educate herself.

Mummy would sometimes visit us in the nursery, but
those occasions were rare. When not in her room, reading, she
was likely to be playing golf or gardening.

Father volunteered for service in the Army in 1916 and
was sent to Camp Lee near Richmond, Virginia. And ever the
dutiful wife, Mummy took a house for us in Richmond to be
close by in early 1917.

One Sunday, Father and his cousin, Alec Rodgers, came

in from the camp to the house on North Frederick Street, a good address in Richmond. They were handsome and dashing in their uniforms. Cousin Alec hugged me and took me into the hall where there was a full–length mirror.

"Let's play monkey faces," he said.

As I looked into the mirror I could see my father behind me, surrounded by an admiring group of ladies who had come by for tea, laughing and flirting. He had neither greeted his children nor asked about them.

I climbed up on the window seat to look out. That, winter was the coldest I could remember. In the park across the street, cascades from the great marble fountain had frozen into circles. Wartime had brought coal shortages, so the house was always chilly. I shivered and slipped away to the nursery.

Father went overseas in May of 1917. At first however, Mummy stayed closed off in her room, crying all day long. But by the next winter she was working with her friends, rolling bandages for the Red Cross.

With the temperatures below freezing, Nanny would wake us to come and see the pictures Jack Frost had painted on the windows, the ice–trees with sparkling branches. Then she would retrieve our woolly underwear from the iron grate in front of the fire. "These panties have gotten nice and warm from the coal fire," she'd say. "It burned all night and I added more coal this morning." I loved drifting off to sleep looking at the glowing coals, and all my life coal fires have made me think of Nanny.

The Armistice was declared in November 1918. A few months later I stood on the balcony of Granny and Grandpa Blair's house in New York, watching the returning troops march up Fifth Avenue. I looked for Father, but I couldn't see him in the mass of khaki–clad soldiers. After a while Father came home, still handsome in his uniform. But he had no time for, or any interest, in his children.

One Sunday soon after, I went into my mother's bedroom. I was dressed for church and for Sunday luncheon at my Clark grandparents. Father was still in bed, reading the paper. Mummy was at her rose–skirted dressing table. Near her was the bunch of violets that she would pin on her muff when she went out. The bottles on her dressing table held an assortment of perfumes. Muguet Des Bois, lily of the valley, was her favorite.

After an elaborate beauty regime of creams and lotions, Mummy took a big powder puff and patted powder on her face. Then she applied lipstick.

"Mummy, will you put some lipstick on me?" I asked.

"Heavens no, dear. I don't want you to be vain. Beauty is as beauty does," she replied.

After watching a little longer, I said, "I can't wait to see Grandpa Clark. I love to hear his stories."

Father put his paper down and looked at Mummy. "I don't want the children tagging along to Sunday lunch."

I ran out of the room before they could see the tears in my eyes, and after we came back from the Madison Avenue Presbyterian Church I watched from the window as my parents walked toward 68th Street. That night I had a dream. Father hadn't come back from the war alive. I saw him laid out in a coffin in his uniform, masses of red roses and white lilies all around him.

After Father came home from the war, Mummy seemed ill much of the time. In December 1920, her diary recorded that she spent twelve days in bed. Dr. Voorhees, her obstetrician, visited daily. Trained nurses attended her. Father, probably unknowingly, had brought home syphilis from France and given it to her.

Marriage to my father had changed Mummy. She was very different from the happy young woman who had married Father and even from the melancholy one who waited for him to return from the war. She was remote, unhappy, and very ill. Her moods swung erratically. No one was spared, not even Nanny. She had always called her Mary, but now she referred to her as "Nurse Grant." When Nanny went to New York from our summer home in Bernardsville on her day off, Mummy wrote in her diary that she was unhappy about being "on duty" with her children.

In early October 1922, Mummy went to look for a governess. Later that month she called me to her room where I was introduced to a tall woman, a Mam'selle Gottreux, from Switzerland. She was not in the least like Nanny.

"Anne," Mummy told me, "Nanny is leaving. Mam'selle Gottreux will be your governess from now on. She will continue the French Mam'selle Figuet taught you at school."

I remember that day; the color of the carpet, which was violet, suddenly turned gray for me. The color went out of the pink chintz curtains as well.

"Nanny is going away? But why?" I asked. My eyes filled with tears. "Nanny loves us, and we love her."

Mummy, reclining on her chaise lounge, didn't move a muscle, but just stared at me. Then she said, as if she had just thought of an excuse: "Oh, Nanny is too untidy."

I ran to the nursery to find Nanny. She was in her own small room, sitting on the bed, disconsolate. I threw myself into her arms, and we cried together.

"Will you write to me, Nanny?" I cried onto her shoulder.

"Your Mummy has forbidden me to write you," Nanny whispered, and my heart stopped. "I must do what she says. She wants you to forget me."

"I'll never forget you, Nanny, never. I'll always love you, forever and ever."

Nanny packed slowly as I sat and watched. She had one good blue dress for her days off. The blue matched her eyes.

She took off her white uniform and hung it in the closet. She pulled on the blue dress and dark stockings, and put on her good black shoes.

"Would you like to brush my hair?" she asked. I brushed her long dark hair for the last time. She twisted it into a knot at the back of her head and put on her blue hat. I clung to her for a last hug. I heard Mummy's voice calling in an agitated tone, "Anne, come here. Come to my room at once."

Nanny opened the front door. Painter, the chauffeur, was waiting to take her to the station. She stepped into the car and waved good–bye. The car drove away, with Nanny blowing kisses.

I climbed the stairs to my mother's room. I never saw Nanny again.

After Nanny had gone, Mummy often described my behavior as very disobedient. For months after Nanny left, there were many spankings. Mummy turned me over her knee and spanked me with a hairbrush or a slipper, always saying, "This hurts me more than it hurts you."

My principal crime was reading. Nanny had taught me to read, and I loved books. But under Mummy's regime, until I turned fourteen, I had to take a long nap every day after lunch. We children were expected to lie absolutely still at nap time, even if we could not sleep, and I could not. In my room in the New York apartment, a circular bookcase stood between my canopied bed and the window. It held all of my favorite books. To reach them, I had to tiptoe out of bed as quietly as a mouse. I did this nearly every day.

I felt that everything I did was wrong. One fall weekend in Bernardsville, I was out in the cornfield with Miss Tucker, a nice "gentlewoman" who had been recruited from Bermuda to take care of me. The day was cool but bright and sunny, the cornstalks stacked up in little golden pyramids. Miss Tucker, who was "artistic," gave me some paper and fixed up a paint box and brush. We each started painting the scene before us: the tawny stubble, the cornstalks, and crows flapping lazily over the field.

Mummy came out to see what we were doing. I heard her footsteps rustling the autumn leaves. She was wearing her new russet tailored suit from Bergdorf Goodman, where she ran up high bills. Mummy stood and watched us for a few moments. Then she decided to sit down—right on my open paint box. She jumped up with a shriek. "Why did you put your paints there?" she asked angrily, stomping off down the lane to the house.

I did not understand mental illness then. My mother was depressed and emotionally unbalanced, chiefly because of syphilis and my father. But we didn't know that as children. She was jealous of any woman who caught my father's eye (as many did). She was jealous of Nanny. Perhaps if Mummy had been emotionally and physically stable, she would have understood how much I grieved over Nanny's loss.

My mother's own early upbringing had been strict, even harsh. At the age of four, she was sent to live with her Grandmother Blair, because her mother found her too hard on her younger sister, Florence, the favored child. Being sent away by her own mother must have left an emotional wound that would never heal. Grandmother Blair was an extremely devout, almost fanatical, Calvinist Presbyterian who lived for the missionary activities of her church to which she liberally donated her husband's money. Every morning at six, my mother was required to join her grandmother for two hours of Bible reading before breakfast. On Sundays, reading the Bible or other religious books was the only acceptable activity.

My mother's grandmother taught her about God, but something, perhaps my mother's own experience in the First World War and her isolation from my father and her own

family, may have caused her to waiver in her faith. In raising
her own children, she adopted the same harsh rules and strict
discipline that prevailed in her childhood. Duty and obedience
were her primary objectives in training her children. She
believed in corporal punishment and often spoke about the
necessity of curbing the spirits of children. "It is like breaking
a horse to bridle," she said, and Mummy was an expert
horsewoman, so she should have known.

I suppose it worked, in its own way. I grew into a dutiful
and obedient child. My brother Blair, always a pragmatic
politician—and Mummy's favorite—also quickly learned that
giving in was the best way to appease her. But my brother
Willie, later called Bill, the middle child, was different, made
of sterner stuff. He would not pretend to be sorry when he
was not. One summer in Hot Springs, Virginia, where we went
every summer, Bill, age 7, spent three days in his room living
on bread and water after he was banished by Mummy for
some mischief. On the third day I pleaded with her to forgive
him.

"Please, Mummy," I begged, imagining Bill miserable
and starving in his room.

"Not until he apologizes," she replied.

That night I listened from my bed to the chant of a
bird, "Whip poor Will, Whip poor Will."

Mummy's discipline did not waver, but its effects were
far reaching, more than she intended. I loved my mother in a
distant and dutiful fashion and I recognized now how much
I needed her. When I was eight years old, she lost a baby
and nearly died herself; after that, I prayed for many nights:
"Please God, let Mummy live until I grow up." It took me a
long time to grow up. As I grew older, I tried to understand
her better, hoping we could grow closer. But, until the day she
died, I was never able to stop being afraid of her.

Mummy was difficult, but she was at least a constant

presence in our lives. Father, on the other hand, was the absent parent of whom we knew so little and whom we never came to know as a person. In 1923, when I was nine, we moved to Princeton. When Blair contracted polio, Mummy took him to Boston to a specialist. They were gone for months, and Willie and I were miserable. We never saw our father. Our grandmothers and great aunts took over to some extent and a sourpuss, Mademoiselle Letlelier, was in charge. What a dreary woman she was.

Around this time there were negotiations to appoint Father to the State Court of Errors and Appeals in Trenton. He was seated in November and at 32 years of age, the youngest man to be appointed a judge of that court.

He was a brilliant man, and his career was everything to him. Eventually, everyone began to refer to him as "The Judge." Later he instructed his grandchildren to call him Poppa Judge. But to my brothers and me, he was cold and unapproachable. If Mummy inspired fear, Father evoked outright terror. When we heard his footsteps returning home in the evening, if he returned at all, we would run and hide to avoid his sharp tongue.

Always working, Father did not often come to Hot Springs with us in the summers and seldom joined us for vacations. In 1923, Mummy took Willie, Blair, and me to Europe. We had a good time in Paris and Switzerland. In July, we were scheduled to go to London. From there Willie and Blair were to go to the seashore at Eastbourne. But I was to join Mummy and Father in visiting dear old aunts and cousins in Scotland. I was excited and could hardly wait.

Father joined us in Europe in July and Mummy told him of her plans to take me along to Scotland. I heard them arguing in the next room of the hotel. A few minutes later, Mummy came out, her cheeks streaked with tears.

"Anne your father says that no children are to go to

Scotland," she said. "I'm sorry."

I cried and begged, but to no avail. Father was impatient and cross, and would not listen. So I was packed off to Eastbourne to a boarding house with my brothers. We spent a month there. Mummy and Father visited us for two days, between their trips to Scotland and Ireland.

I wonder now if my father even liked his children. His way was harsh and unkind. As we got older, he was sometimes even overtly cruel. As I entered my teens, he often criticized my appearance. His nickname for me was "the chinless wonder." He frequently suggested I do exercises to enlarge my chin, which was mortifying and painful to me. Though I feared him, I did respect my father's intellect and his position as judge made me proud. I believed his ethics, too, were worthy of respect. It was only much later, when I was grown and married, that I learned of all his philandering. How my mother must have suffered.

Eventually, I learned that since his days at Harvard Father had been an alcoholic. As a judge, however, he personally observed all laws, including Prohibition. During the years 1923 to 1933, alcohol was not served at home, nor did anyone, including Father, drink alcohol. This explained much of Father's bad disposition. Rather than go to speakeasies where he might be recognized, he and his heavy drinking buddies would occasionally take cruise ships to Bermuda where they could drink freely and legally. After Prohibition was repealed, Father made up for the years of deprivation.

When Father did notice his children, he demanded obedience. Many men of his day were like that, but they were at least involved in their children's lives while he was not. Bill, once again, was the only one who finally dared to challenge him; but doing so exacted a tremendous price.

In 1940, World War II was in full swing and both my brothers received their draft announcements early. The Sunday after Bill received his notice he had lunch with our parents in Princeton. He told them that he had been drafted, and that he objected, saying that he didn't believe wars solved anything. My father's face turned beet red and his voice rose. He berated Bill for waiting to be drafted and for not having volunteered. The argument became more heated. Suddenly, Father got up from the table. "Stand up, you dirty slacker," he said to Bill, "defend yourself."

My mother tried to intervene, but in a moment, the two men had exchanged blows. Father was on the floor in a matter of seconds.

"Pack your bags," he said, getting up. "I don't ever want to see a son who's such a coward again."

Bill packed up and left. He eventually enlisted in the Army Air Corps. But he never saw Father alive again. He did go to say good–bye to him at his funeral in Arlington years later.

Bill, perhaps, took things to extremes. But on the other end of the scale, I was too docile, too easily bent to my parents' will. This was partly due to the times, but partly to my nature, my desire to always please and to keep the peace. My inability to stand my ground in the face of my parents— especially my father's expectations—set me on a course that took me away from my living my own life for a long, long time.

Chapter Two

School was my refuge.

Everything was different from what I had known at home. It was the only place, especially after Nanny left, where I felt not only appreciated, but even special.

I learned to read when I was four. Nanny taught me my ABCs and how to count. One day, when Nanny was giving Blair his bottle, I sat on the floor putting blocks together. "Nanny, look, look," I called to her. "That says *dog*!"

"So it does, darlin'." She leaned down and rearranged the blocks. "And this spells *god*." Nanny was a devout Catholic and often would take us to visit the cathedrals in New York City. St. Patrick's at Christmas was our favorite because of the elaborate crèche, or as Nanny would say in wonderment, the "Baby Jesus." I was baptized a Presbyterian, and we went to church every Sunday at Madison Avenue Presbyterian church. Of course, my father would only go on the "high holidays." Mummy enrolled us in Sunday school, but after my father left for Chicago to work on big case, we stopped attending Church. Rather, Mummy would read us from the Bible on Sunday mornings and engage us in discussions. She felt that she could do a better job of giving us our religious education than any church. My faith has sustained me all these years, and I still attend regular services at Trinity Episcopal Church in Princeton.

I entered Lenox School (today it is called The Birch Wathen Lenox School), one of the first Montessori Schools in America, and progressed into the first grade. The teachers there were warm, affectionate and approving, especially

Mam'selle Figuet, the French teacher and my favorite.

She was full of warmth, imagination, and fun. From her, I learned a great deal more than French. One year, soon after Nanny left, she spent an entire summer with us at the house we rented close to my grandparents in Bernardsville, New Jersey. She had full charge of me, since my mother, who was spanking me daily, thought I needed extra attention. Mam'selle Figuet and I walked in the fields together, and she pointed out the dewdrops sparkling among the threads of a spider web in the morning sun. "They look like diamonds on a chain," she said, and suddenly I saw the glittering threads in a different way. Sometimes we walked to a nearby farm where I was allowed to grab the handle of the butter churn and move it up and down, up and down, until specks of butter appeared. Other times we watched the sun "walk" along the woods with us, as Mam'selle would say, or the moon would do the same in the early evening.

Mam'selle's father died before she was born. She came to America to live with an uncle in Ohio. He sent her to college and, after graduating, she made her living teaching French to the children of the very wealthy. Never one to complain, I remember her as *toujours gaie.* For years after we parted, she sent me postcards from a magical mountain land, Keene Valley in the Adirondacks, where she spent her summers working at the Community House. When I finally went there for the first time, more than 30 years later, the mountain landscape seemed oddly familiar. Mam'selle and I did meet again when I was an adult. She came to visit me in New York when I was a newlywed and spent most of our visit telling me how sorry she felt for me when I was growing up. She had loved me so, she said.

In 1922, the year I turned eight, Mummy was not feeling well and did nothing about sending my brothers or me to school. Instead, she hired the horrid English Miss Stevens as our governess to see to our education. Miss Stevens forbade us to read during nap time or after lights out. She spied on us and reported our indiscretions to Mummy. Oh, how we hated her. It seems our lives that winter were made up of nothing more than lessons with Miss Stevens and occasional trips to a gym for exercise.

But after we moved to Princeton in 1923, I was enrolled in Miss Fine's School, where I flourished. Miss Stevens continued to be in charge at home, but my academic performance inspired her to treat me with more respect. At the end of the school year, my mother called us in to tell us that she planned to write a glowing report to Miss Stevens' training school in London. We listened, incredulous, as she described our governess in terms more appropriate to an angel from heaven. Later, when we were back upstairs, I asked Willie and Blair what they thought of Mummy's letter.

"She doesn't see how awful Miss Stevens is," Willie said.

"It is no use telling her," I replied. "I've tried. She won't listen."

"We just have to hope she does something awful and Mummy finds out about it." Blair said.

And finally Miss Stevens obliged. One night she stayed out too late on a date, leaving Blair imprisoned for four hours in the braces he had to wear for polio, instead of the suggested two hours. Mummy took her to task for her irresponsibility, but she still hesitated to dismiss her. Miss. Stevens eventually left the next year.

I continued in Miss Fine's School through the eighth grade. Miss Fine herself taught me Latin one–on–one because I was far ahead of my classmates in most subjects. Miss Fine, usually dressed in black bombazine with a white collar and cuffs and with her white hair piled on top of her head, knew how to make Latin exciting. She was a remarkable teacher and I loved her school, even though it took some time for me to find acceptance there. For a long time, just because I was the new girl, no one played with me during recess. At first, only the boys liked me. But gradually the girls, too, came around, and I found that I was actually popular.

We were spending the summer in Hot Springs, Virginia, when I turned 14 and Mummy summoned me to her room.

"Anne, your father and I have decided that you should go to boarding school. You will go to St. Timothy's, near Baltimore, where I went."

I didn't understand why I had to leave home, but my mother explained that she and Father felt that Princeton, as a university town, was not a good place for a teenage girl.

"You say that because Mary, who lives down the block, got pregnant?" I asked with a flash of daring. "But I won't," I insisted.

Mummy waived her hand dismissively. "Just on general principles," she said.

There was no further discussion. When we returned to Princeton, Mummy directed Mimi to pack my trunk with school uniforms and a few other belongings. Painter, our chauffeur, drove us down to Catonsville, Maryland, in the maroon Lincoln. St. Timothy's was founded in the 1880s to educate young ladies of "good" families by two Southern gentlewomen, the Misses Carter, whose goal was to bring together girls from the North and the South to help heal the wounds of the Civil War. It was in the lap of the Episcopal Church of the same name. The church was an integral part of life at the school. Minister Yardley gave heartfelt and sobering sermons. St. Timothy's, I soon learned, was the equivalent of a convent; its rules were strict and confining.

At the entrance, we were besieged by two large groups of girls. One group was clad all in green, the other in brown. The green group stood on one side of the car as we drove by chanting "Spider, spider, spider." The other group shouted

Brownie, brownie, brownie."

"They want you to choose one of the athletic groups," Mummy explained. "You'll have to be a Spider because I was."

Of course.

Mummy was clearly delighted to be back at the school where she had spent three happy years. In her day, the Misses Carter ran the school. In my era, Miss Fowler, a humorless disciplinarian, was headmistress.

"I hope you are just like your mother," Miss Fowler said as she greeted me. She looked me over carefully. "Perhaps you're not," she said.

Miss Fowler introduced me to one of my roommates, Charlotte, a cheerful, bouncy girl from Boston. Charlotte took me up to our room on the second floor of the old red wooden building. There I met my other roommate, Elizabeth, a beautiful, rather remote girl. Crowded into our small room were three beds, three bureaus, and three straight-back chairs. In the corner was a table holding a pitcher and basin.

Charlotte turned to the door and pointed at a printed page mounted on the back. "Those are the school rules," she said. "You had better study them." It looked to me as though there were at least a hundred rules.

Charlotte pointed to one she said was very important:

DO NOT SIT ON THE BED

"The head teacher inspects our rooms every morning," Charlotte explained. "You have to have a smooth bed and all your things put away."

Charlotte's warm, motherly attitude helped to assuage the ache in my heart. I missed my friends at Miss Fine's, none of whom had to go to boarding school.

Indeed, St Timothy's did have a myriad of rules. One I learned quickly was the all-important communication rule. Students were not allowed to talk to one another after the bell

rang in the daytime at the beginning of classes, or at night
when the bell rang for bedtime. If we broke any rule, we had
to publicly confess. Every rule broken earned an X mark,
called a "cross," in a ledger that Miss Fowler brought to study
hall every day. A "cross" could be worked off by walking the
length of the school's driveway a prescribed number of times,
or "walking the lane" as it was ominously referred to.

Every night, we girls were expected to troop past Miss
Fowler's chair to kiss her goodnight. I found that to be an
unpleasant encounter, due to the prickly hair on her chin and
her tendency to greet me with comments such as, "Anne, why
do you have to study with your hair? It gets so messy. Oh dear,
I wish you were more like your mother."

No boys were allowed to visit or even telephone. Any
letter one of us might receive from a boy was registered in
Miss Fowler's book. The recipient was then called to her
office, known as the "cupboard," where she had to hand over
the letter to Miss Fowler to read. The reply had to be placed,
unsealed, into a bowl for her to review before it could be sent.

There were no classes and no studying on Sundays.
The only reading material permitted was the Bible or other
religious books. Many students went to church at eight in the
morning, sang hymns at ten in the school living room, and
then attended a second church service at eleven. There were
also evening prayers at five in the afternoon. We somehow
survived. We ate meals at long tables in the dining room,
served by black maids in frilly white caps. The milk was
skimmed blue, but the food was very Southern and very good:
biscuits with butter, spoon bread, and sometimes homemade
ice cream.

I liked sitting at the "French" table with Mademoiselle
Soubigou who thought my French accent was quite good.
She, and the other teachers, were maiden ladies of uncertain
age who were paid—so the rumor went—a token salary. If

this was true, it was scandalous, for most of them were good teachers.

One day, Miss Harper, who taught history, called me in to her classroom after an examination. "Anne, I am puzzled by your exam paper," she said. "You've repeated word for word five pages of the book."

Miss Harper admitted, somewhat uneasily, that I could not have taken the book into the exam room with me, as she had checked everyone. "I suppose you must have a photographic memory," she said.

My visual memory was undeniably one of the reasons why I did well in school. My auditory memory, however, was very poor. Mummy complained that I didn't listen to her. I tried, but I could not retain much of anything I heard. In class, I always took voluminous notes. One year, while at St. Timothy's, Mummy wrote me: "You may not have heard the announcement at Prize Day; you led the entire school. We are very proud of you." It was a rare word of praise from my parents and I cherished it.

My contact with the outside world was limited to the front page of the *New York Times*. This was the only page of the paper Miss Fowler allowed us to read. It was tacked up on the bulletin board daily. This was disconcerting to me. Since the age of nine, I had read some of the *Times* every day aloud to my mother while she ate breakfast in bed, wearing her pink bed jacket.

While I was at St. Timothy's, President Coolidge appointed my father to the federal district court in Newark. I was told that once again he was the youngest judge ever appointed at that level. One morning in 1930, I began reading an account of my father's ruling that the Volstead Act, which instituted Prohibition, was unconstitutional. [The ruling, although subsequently overturned by the Supreme Court, had a wide-ranging impact on the issue of state's rights.] The

Times had run the story on page one, right–hand column, where the important news story of the day was printed (and continues to be to this day). But the story continued on an inside page —and I was not allowed to read it.

In my final year, we put on "A Midsummer's Night's Dream." I played Bottom, and Kate Emmet was Puck. But the week before graduation, when the play was to be presented, Kate developed bronchitis. I visited her in the infirmary.

"Kate," I told her, "you must get well. If you don't get up to play Puck, Miss Elmore says she'll do it." Miss Elmore was our English teacher and dramaturge.

"Anything but that," responded Kate. She jumped out of bed and recovered just in time to play a splendid Puck.

On a spring day toward the end of my final year, six of us sat around a table, talking about the future and what we would do when school was over. "My parents want me to come back to Erie and come out," said Kate, and we all groaned, knowing that we faced the same dreadful fate – becoming debutantes. It was what our parents expected.

Then Mary piped up, "Let's go to college."

We sat silently for a moment. "How about Smith College?" Kate cried all at once. "My aunt lives near there."

This was during the depression, and even though St. Timothy's was for proper girls, i.e. wealthy, several were forced to leave school because of financial hardship. And Smith College at that time, with tuition of $1000 per year, was still out of reach for many. So, for those of us who knew our parents could afford it, Smith didn't seem out of reach. Mummy, uncertain, went to Northampton, Massachusetts, to look at the campus. She told the dean that Father thought I should come out and go to parties so that I could meet a suitable young man, get married, and settle down. Father, like most of the fathers of my friends, thought all a college education would do was make me unfit to be a wife and mother, the only future for a girl like me.

But somehow, Father was convinced to indulge me. He let me postpone my coming out for a year so that I could attend Smith. I could hardly believe it. I was going to be a college girl!

In September 1932, my mother drove my friend Mary Rogers and me to Northampton to begin our freshman year at Smith. With two other St. Timothy's girls, Kate Emmett and Carolyn Gay, we would live across the street from the main campus on Henshaw Avenue, in a wood–shingled house that came complete with maids to make up the beds. My mother helped us unpack and pulled out the colorful bedspreads and cushions she had brought to bring along to brighten our room.

Then Mummy drove back to Princeton, full of misgivings that she confided in her diary. She had never gone to college and felt it was probably unnecessary and possibly dangerous for me to go. She feared I could develop into an "intellectual woman," a kind of repulsive creature who wore spectacles, dressed in frumpish clothing, and expressed opinions about matters that should be no concern of women, such as politics. She was also worried that my chances of making a successful marriage would be hindered by a college education. Yet, maybe because she was denied the opportunity, she felt that my achievement in academic pursuits should be recognized.

My mother read voraciously, to make up for her lack of a formal education, and to keep apace with my father. She developed a very keen mind and an ardent intellectual curiosity, deeply interested in history, especially the civil war and religion. She would pursue these interests quite passionately in later years, ironically becoming a true intellectual woman.

My parents may have been agonizing, but I was reveling

in my newfound freedom. I was excited by everything—the
courses I chose, the stimulating professors, meeting new
people, and making new friends. I had liked St. Timothy's
most of the time, but now, for the first time, I was meeting
young women who came from different backgrounds.

One evening at our house, a group of girls started
talking about the meals they had at home and what they
missed about their mothers' cooking. One of them turned to
me and said, "What about you, Anne? What did your mother
cook that you especially loved?"

I was thunderstruck—and on the spot. I was too
embarrassed to explain that my mother couldn't even boil
an egg, much less prepare an entire meal. At home, we
children had never been allowed to set foot in the kitchen.
A tyrannical cook, who made meals of Cordon Bleu quality
but terrorized Mummy and the rest of us, ruled the kitchen.
Mummy, of course, ordered the meals, but that was as far as
her involvement with them extended. I couldn't bring myself
to confess any of this, so I stammered out a feeble response,
"Chocolate cake." Mummy never made a cake in her life. I
actually found a copy of *How to Cook A Fried Egg* amongst
my mother's papers when she died.

I was happier at Smith than I had been since my days
with Nanny, wandering around the campus in the schoolgirl
uniform of the day—Bermuda tweed skirts in a pastel color,
matching Shetland sweaters buttoned up the back, a leather
belt and a discreet necklace of pearls, and of course the
ubiquitous white saddle shoes with black or brown leather
trim. It was fashionable to let the white part of the shoe
become rather gray. We looked like paper doll cutouts.

At Smith, no one criticized me or corrected me or
made me feel, as I did at home, that everything I said or did
was wrong or stupid. I found for the first time that what I
said, what I wrote, what I thought, and what I felt, really

mattered.

When we first arrived at Smith, none of my friends from St. Timothy's nor I were thirsting for knowledge. We thought college would be more of a social experience, a mere extension of our boarding school. But for me, this quickly changed. Exposed to people who loved ideas and loved discussing them, I discovered I felt the same way.

I kept a diary in which I recorded the speeches and lectures that impressed me. The author Mary Ellen Chase was a professor of English literature whose course I hoped to take my sophomore year. I attended a lecture she gave, titled, "What Makes Literature Good?" "Power," she revealed, "ideas and expression, beauty and truth." I found her ideas fascinating, but in my diary I wrote, "She read poetry abominably."

T. S. Eliot spoke on the poetry of Edward Lear. With several friends, I went to hear Felix Frankfurter speak. He later became a Supreme Court justice. One of my classmates insisted he was probably a Communist because of the role he had played as attorney for the defense in the notorious Sacco and Vanzetti case in the late 1920s.

Professor Welsh taught music and lectured on the performances for the student body. He discussed Beethoven's Third Symphony, and the recurring themes in Wagner's "Siegfried." I knew a little about music because Mummy, who loved Wagner, had occasionally taken me to concerts and operas. But she had little interest in either poetry or art, and the judge, of course, had no interest in anything but politics and the law, so the small art gallery at Smith was a revelation. Picasso hit me between the eyes. I was not sure at all what to make of him. In my diary, I wrote that his "*Seated Woman* was the most amazing thing I have ever seen. They say that it is one of the great paintings of the twentieth century. I'm sorry for the century, but I suppose I must be reactionary or dumb."

My exploration of the world, writ large, was beginning.
I loved the European History course taught by Professor
Scramuzza. The gossip was that he was a radical, perhaps
even a Communist. As a text, he used Bernard Fay's
The Underlying Causes of the World War, which was very
influential at the time. Professor Scramuzza agreed with
Fay that selfish business interests and the cartels were the
primary causes of the Great War, for they had profited at
the expense of their countries. As for the press, he declared
it irresponsible, stirring up nationalistic feelings that stoked
the fires of conflict. Although I didn't have strong political
views then, I knew I didn't feel quite the same way as many
of my conservative friends at Smith. The world was changing
in 1932. It was the third year of the Great Depression.
Unemployed men were selling apples on street corners,
or traveling on foot between New York and Philadelphia,
looking for work and begging door to door for a cup of soup
or something to eat. They would come to the back door of our
house in Princeton and knock, asking if they could rake the
yard or sweep the steps. My mother's instructions to our cook
were to let her know right away if anyone came to the door
looking for a meal. And when summoned, my mother would
come to the kitchen (which she seldom otherwise entered) and
give orders for a meal to be given first. And then she would
slip the poor man a little cash in his hands and wish him well.

Mummy wrote to tell me of a man who came to our
door who fell in a dead faint on the kitchen floor. The maid ran
up to her room, all in a tizzy. She hurried down in her dressing
gown to the kitchen and when he opened his eyes, my mother
asked him when he had last eaten. "Four days ago," was all he
could say. After that incident, Mummy organized part of the
garage as a sort of soup kitchen. Eventually, she persuaded

Trinity Church and other local churches in Princeton to take over. She was always generous, even when she ran up heavy debts for extravagant clothes and beautiful furniture. She bought most of her clothes from "Mr. Bergdorf" and even during the depression, he told her that he could wait indefinitely for payment, because he knew she would pay him sooner or later.

When I got to Smith, Franklin Roosevelt was running for President on the Democratic ticket promising to restore prosperity. It was the first time I was really aware of a presidential election.

My father knew Roosevelt as they both went to Harvard and were members of the same club there, although not at the same time. And although father was a Republican and my mother became a Democrat, they both enthusiastically supported Roosevelt.

By 1932, various plans were being made to turn the economy around and events in Europe loomed large. At Smith I joined a number of clubs and organizations that today would be described as liberal. Dr. Raymond Fosdick of Riverside Church had a daughter at Smith and he spoke at one more of our chapel services. He spoke eloquently about the plight of so many, once happy now destitute, once gainfully employed now begging for an hour of yard work. We were aware that people were poor and hungry, that men on Wall Street had thrown themselves out of windows, that former Bank presidents were on the street. But Smith was still a very sheltered environment, an extension of a girl's boarding school for privileged young women. The problems of the real world didn't come too close to us.

There were a few girls at Smith who could not afford the full tuition, so they worked as maids and waitresses in our campus houses. How strong those girls must have been, to be our classmates as well as our servants.

Although I was still too young to vote, I tacked a large poster of Roosevelt up in the hall every day. Each night it disappeared.

"What awful girl is stealing my poster?" I complained to my roommate Mary. Mary was a staunch Republican, but I never suspected her. Much later, she told me that it was she who in fact stole and destroyed the posters every night. However different politically, Mary and I were aberrations. Most of the girls were completely indifferent to the campaign. On election night, Kate invited me to go along with her to the movies. I was horrified.

"Aren't you going to listen to the returns on the radio?" I asked her.

"What returns?" Kate asked.

I wrote to Granny Clark: "The Smith girls are so dumb. They can't think for themselves and are for the candidate their parents like."

Granny wrote back, "Aren't you?"

My parents were delighted with Roosevelt's victory. "We believe Roosevelt will save our country," Mummy wrote me, and later, when FDR was inaugurated in March, she sent me a detailed description of the inauguration.

Then the President closed the banks. Mummy, with her usual foresight, had placed a considerable amount of cash in her safety deposit box, so she had funds for herself and enough to lend to friends. The situation in the country was very tense, but my parents had faith in Roosevelt. Many of my friends and their parents considered him a traitor to his (read "our") class, but I admired him and he gave me the feeling that he was in charge. Still, after the banks closed, I wrote in my diary: "These may be thrilling times, but I could do without some of the thrills."

I went home at Easter, where I noted that Mummy looked ill and seemed hardly to sleep even with the aid of pills. I guessed she was worried about money.

"I am planning my courses for next year," I said to my parents about the various classes I hoped to take as a sophomore. Then I told them what I had been thinking about and planning for the long run. It seemed so natural to me. I wanted to major in government, and "I'm thinking of going to law school after college," I announced. "I'd really like to be a lawyer." I looked at my father expectantly, waiting for his pleased reaction to the news that his only daughter wished to follow in his footsteps.

My father stopped eating. He looked at my mother in consternation. Then he threw down his napkin and rose from the table.

"That's an absurd idea. I cannot imagine why your mother encouraged you to attend Smith. Or why, in God's name, you would want to attend law school when you should be trying to get married. Assuming anyone suitable wants you," my father growled.

I was devastated, but I went back to Smith and put the memory of the scene behind me. In May, my social life at Smith reached an apex when I was asked to join the Orangemen, a secret society of which it was a privilege to be a member. Only twelve girls in each class were honored with an invitation, and I was the only St. Timothy's girl who received one. I had mixed feelings: the idea of a secret society seemed frivolous to me, but at the same time, I was flattered. The invitation came in the form of a note from an upperclassman who addressed me as "Clark, you cloistered carbuncle," and proceeded to dispense instructions for me to "run" or wait on two older girls, to wear a baby's cap, and other rather juvenile procedures. I did it all, except the final trial—performing a skit on initiation night. I escaped that ordeal by going to the infirmary with the flu—self-induced. So I did not join the Orangemen in the end.

Over the summer, our family usually retreated to Hot Springs., Virginia. George Cole Scott, scion of a prominent Richmond family, was there. George Cole's father had recently died and left him $10,000 a year, which meant he could support a wife in considerable style. In today's dollars, that's approximately $150,000 a year. My parents were not unaware of this. They pushed me hard in George Cole's direction, just as his family seemed to push him in mine. But I was not ready for a serious romance. I was going back to school in the fall, after all.

One morning, Mummy called me to her room. She was sitting up in bed, sipping coffee, her breakfast tray perched on her knees. We had learned never to speak to her before her cup of coffee had steadied her volatile temper.

"Your father and I have been discussing what you should do this year," she said at last.

I was surprised and didn't understand. "But, of course, I'm going back to Smith," I said, "I can't wait."

Mummy was silent for a moment. Then she said, "No, we don't think you should."

I was stunned. What did she mean? But all I could eke out was a feeble, "Why not?"

Mummy began to talk about how she and Father were afraid that I was becoming too much of an intellectual, that I was too serious, that I should take a year off and be a debutante, come out at a ball, and go to parties. I listened, but I could hardly hear her; it was as though she was talking to me from a very long distance away.

I tried to tell her how much I loved Smith, how I could go to parties there, go to Harvard on the weekends and have a wonderful time and meet lots of young men. But she hardly listened.

"As we don't know these young men or their parents, it is not the same thing, my dear," she said. I knew it was futile.

I was dismissed.

I went to my room and paced the floor in anger and confusion, wondering if my clothes allowance would stretch far enough to cover the Smith tuition. I had no experience and no one to guide me. Years later, I found out that Granny Clark disapproved of my parents' decision and had been arguing with them over taking me out of college. Had I known I had an ally, perhaps my future would have been different. All of it. My whole life.

For days, I continued to argue with my mother. I was too angry to cry, but I felt helpless and hopeless before the steel wall that was her will. My father, I was sure, had much to do with her decision, but he was never around and could never be confronted. I probably would have been much too frightened to confront him anyway.

All summer long Mummy put pressure on me to withdraw from Smith. Finally in August, I gave in. I wrote the warden, the Smith official who dealt with enrollment and withdrawal.

I set down the words. "I withdraw from Smith," knowing full well that I was withdrawing from a path I yearned to follow. On August 14, 1933, Joy Secor the registrar at Smith wrote me at Hot Springs. "I am sorry to hear that you are not planning to return to Smith this coming year. I assume from your letter that it is because of family plans rather than because of finances. If it were the latter reason I should have been glad to try to find a solution." What a wonderful offer, in the midst of the depression, but I lacked the courage to challenge my parents' will. It would take me many decades to start on that path again.

Chapter Three

Love.

No one had looked harder for it, longed for it more than I. But ever since love left with Nanny, I was afraid it would never come to me again, that natural, open love that signifies understanding and unconditional acceptance. I knew I would never have that kind of supportive, all–encompassing love I would have wished from my parents. But I was aware by now that there were other kinds of love. This was exciting and frightening at once.

I was aware of boys and played with lots of them in the park. They all admired my bright red scooter. After taking a spin on it, one of them, John, invited me to play baseball with the boys.

"Do other girls play?" I asked.

"No, they're scaredy–cats," John replied in a voice full of disdain. "But you're not. You can play shortstop."

"What's a shortstop?" I asked.

Bertie, who also coveted my scooter, lived across the street and often came to parties with my brothers and me. These were usually elaborate affairs with magic shows, Punch and Judy, or single–reel Charlie Chaplin movie flickering in black and white. Sometimes there were costume parties. Once I went as Little Bo Beep, in a blue satin dress with panniers on either side. Mummy said that "pannier" was French for baskets. Bertie went as Robin Hood, with a rakish green cap.

"I have something to show you," Bertie whispered during the movie. "Come into the hall."

We tiptoed out to a dark corner, where Bertie proudly

opened his fly and pulled his penis out of his pants.

"Oh, that," I said, unimpressed. "My little brothers have those."

By the time I got to Smith, my father really had nothing to support his fears that I would become too intellectual. He would have realized this if he could have read my diary. In it I wrote endlessly about the young men I fancied I was in love with, which I had met either through family or the weekend parties at Harvard and elsewhere that I attended with my friends. "When will N. write?" I moaned in its pages, or "J. has written a wonderful letter." Clothes and boys seemed to be my chief preoccupations.

I wrote my observations about the opposite sex: "All boys are alike," I declared, and "they all like girls." But later, a little more subtlety and confusion crept into my thoughts. When I went home to Princeton at Easter, I hoped to see Neddie, my true love of the moment. He was not very tall, but blond and good–looking, and I believed he had a poetic soul. But I sensed he was not very interested in girls, at least not yet. "I'm beginning to change my mind," I wrote. "When I analyze my feelings dispassionately, I know I'm not really in love. It is indiscreet to write in my diary, but I've got to tell someone."

All the freshmen at Smith were required to take the hygiene course, which was a rather primitive precursor to today's sex education classes. It discussed the reproductive system. In my diary, I noted: "The textbook for my hygiene course takes all the joy out of life. It says all love is founded on sexual desire, and—oh horrible!—age 22 is called 'Searching for the Mate.' Honestly! I guess I must be Victorian."

After I turned eighteen, Mummy was single–minded in her determination that I find a suitable mate. In my parents' mind, my year at Smith was only a temporary diversion

from what must be my primary task, finding a husband.
The social round began immediately after I came home from
Northampton. My friend Carolyn Gay, from New Orleans,
came to Princeton with her parents for her brother Eddie's
graduation, and I was invited to some of the balls and other
festivities.

"You have my permission to marry Eddie Gay,"
Mummy declared to me. I could only laugh.

"He hasn't asked me—and what's more he's engaged," I
replied.

Most of the young men my parents considered
"suitable" I did not find interesting, including George Cole
Scott, with whom I was thrown together with a vengeance
at Hot Springs, Virginia, that summer. When my mother
organized a dinner party of young people at our house, she
placed George Cole on my right. I talked to him through
dinner—or rather, I listened. He never stopped talking. The
following night, George's mother invited all of us for dinner
and the movies at the Homestead, the hotel that was the
queen of the valley and the center of all activities there. After
the movies, there was dancing. George Cole "dances divinely"
I recorded, and he told me he thought I was attractive. But
he had such a line; I didn't dare believe a word he said. I told
Mummy, who agreed that he may well say the same sort of
thing to every girl he meets. "That's the way of Southern
men," Mummy said.

Nevertheless, I was itching to return to Smith, and
Mummy's thunderbolt announcement that I was not to
go back all but destroyed me. Though Mummy was the
messenger, I knew in my heart that the real decision maker
was my father. He and I never talked about it—the Judge did
not discuss anything with me. As far as he was concerned,
I was less than a wallflower; I was the wallpaper. He talked
to my mother or his friends in my presence without ever

including me in the conversation.

Yet I knew, because Mummy told me, how desperate he was for me to attract a good husband, and not merely for the usual economic and familial reasons. For my father, social success was profoundly important. As a teenager, he had been shy and awkward with girls. Although he had a married a Blair, whose family was one of Mrs. Astor's 400, he believed the Clark name lacked the same social standing. Now he wanted to be able to boast to his friends that his daughter was the belle of the ball. When he and Mummy attended some of the balls I went to in New York, he would sit in the balcony and count the young men who danced with me. No matter how many there were, it was never enough. He made this abundantly clear to me. He didn't seem to grasp that humiliating me was not the best way to motivate me through this process that I bitterly resented.

I mourned when Smith opened in the fall without me. I missed the classes, my friends, the professors, the challenge, and the freedom. I read Shelley's "Ode to the West Wind" and wished that the west wind would blow me away.

Mummy bribed me with lots of pretty dresses from Bergdorf Goodman. I had nothing to do but to show off the new clothes at the debutante lunches and teas that Mummy made sure I attended. I couldn't imagine anything more boring. Mummy, in fact, was in her element, planning a dinner dance for my coming out with Miss Cutting, a lady who supported herself by acting as a debutante consultant, handling young women as if we were fillies training for a race. As indeed we were—the marriage race.

Early in September, the round of debutante dances began. I was invited to a dance at Drumthwacket, the Pyne family residence, and later the New Jersey governor's mansion in Princeton. My escort was John, my favorite Princetonian. He was musical and played the piano very well. He had auburn hair and a whimsical smile. We walked in the starlight and he kissed me. My first kiss. Instantly, I fancied I was madly in love with him. I knew my mother would find him suitable. But, in fact, he was only in his second year of college, a boy of nineteen. Marriage for a boy that young would be several years away. Father and Mummy did not encourage that romance.

Marjorie Goodman, my dear friend from St. Timothy's, got married in Lake Forest that fall. I was a bridesmaid. We wore satin dresses in a symphony of autumn colors. One of the ushers, a tall, good–looking blonde gave me a big rush. I found him attractive and imagined myself falling in love. But like many of the boys I met there, he drank too much. Perhaps it was a reaction to my father's drinking, but I did not approve.

When I returned to Hot Springs, George Cole Scott and two of his friends arrived for a weekend. George invited me to Richmond, Virginia, to visit the Scott family mansion, Ballyshannon. His mother, Hildreth, was actually from Massachusetts, but upon marrying a Southerner had become the consummate Southern Belle, which my mother found "silly." I drove to Richmond with Mrs. Christian, a friend of Mummy's, and two other ladies. They gossiped cattily along the way about the social circles in Richmond. Mrs. Christian told me I had George Cole "in the bag," but there were many other attractive young men I should meet.

They dropped me at Ballyshannon, the Scott residence. The weekend went well, and on Sunday George drove me to Claremont, one of the lovely James River mansions. As we walked the grounds, he turned and kissed me, and surprised, I found myself kissing back. Later, I confided to my diary: "He kissed me. Of course, I thought I'd have more will power...I love him, I guess, although I wonder." I thought no nice girl kissed a man unless she was really in love with him.

In October, I attended the Tuxedo Autumn Ball and a
tea in Tuxedo Park for my cousin, Joan Blair. George Cole flew
up to join me. The next day, after he went fox hunting in Far
Hills, we drove to Princeton. That night, he told me he loved
me. I was startled. I hadn't expected him to be serious yet. I
was not really sure of myself. But, the next day, after supper,
he was insistent. I wrote in my diary: "He made me say I
loved him and then asked me to marry him."

I was torn between excitement and fear. George wanted
to marry within the year. This seemed too fast to me. I was
flattered and bewildered at once. I half–talked myself into
believing this was what I really wanted. This was love at last,
I thought.

But part of me felt nagging unquiet. Was this truly
what I wanted? I was nineteen, going on sixteen. How could I
be certain? I was somewhat reassured, though, by the thought
that Mummy would no doubt oppose too hasty a wedding.
She believed I was too young to actually marry yet. Her own
thinking had been to use the debutante round to entice a
young man, have us see each other for a year or two as was
often customary, and then arrange a marriage. But to my
surprise and chagrin, she did not object when I told her that
George wanted us to marry soon.

My next meeting with George was at Elk Mountain, the
Scott family retreat near Charlottesville, Virginia, and George
suggested going for a lovely walk overlooking the Blue Ridge
Mountains. It was near sunset and the horizon was flaming
as if the world was on fire. A few copper leaves still hung on
the branches of the mountains' majestic oaks. We paused in
our stroll, and George shyly took a ring out of his pocket. It
was his grandmother's ring, an Oriental pearl set between two
diamonds. He gently placed it on the fourth finger of my left
hand. I gazed at the ring and then kissed him lightly.

Events followed upon another precipitously. Not long

after giving me the ring, George flew north to formally ask the Judge for my hand in marriage. Dinner was strained that evening. For once, George Cole sat in silence, pale and tense, while my father ate without a word. When we finally finished what seemed like an interminable meal, Mummy indicated to me to follow her upstairs while Father and George headed for the library to talk.

We waited nervously upstairs to be summoned as the two men conversed for an hour and a half. Most of the discussion, George told me later, was about the stock market. George Cole was working in Richmond for a New York stock brokerage firm. He liked his job, even though it was the depths of the Depression and his salary was only $15 a week plus commissions, of which there were few. The Judge, however, looked down on stock brokers, thinking them no better than thieves. By the time the talk turned to marriage, poor George was wound up as tight as a clock with anxiety. But his worries were unfounded. The Judge was ecstatic at the thought that I would be marrying the scion of a First Family of Virginia, a young man with good looks and adequate income. What more could a girl want? In his view, snagging this catch was a far greater success than graduating well from a good college and training to be a lawyer. Now my parents could be satisfied that they had done a good job with their daughter who would be making an eminently suitable marriage right after her debut. Mission accomplished.

We celebrated with champagne toasts. But in the ensuing days, something odd happened. Now that it was too late, Mummy suddenly seemed filled with second thoughts and qualms about the marriage. She tried to put on the brakes, to slow the rush to the altar.

One day I came down the spiral staircase of our house to hear my parents arguing. Mummy was saying I was too young to marry. But the Judge shouted, in a voice loud enough to carry up the stairs: "You had better not stop this marriage. She is so unattractive, no one else will ever propose to her."

Mummy gave in. The engagement was announced in January, the wedding date was set and arrangements were soon underway. Mummy went into high gear and took charge of the preparations, hiring a consultant and drawing up the guest list. The Judge insisted that every politician in New Jersey be invited as he was being urged to run for the U.S. Senate. So, along with family and social friends, the guest list came to more than 1,000 people; most accepted.

As the presents poured in, Mummy and the consultant spent endless hours planning what I should wear. The heirloom lace veil, once worn by Napoleon's sister and which my grandfather had purchased many years ago, was removed from the vault. Mummy took it to a well–known designer in New York who created a tulle dress with a wide skirt to go with it. Some pieces of old family lace were appliquéd on the dress that I found breathtakingly beautiful in spite of myself. As for the veil, it was tortured with wire to form a "Mary Queen of Scots" headdress at my request. I was in a period of romanticism about my Scottish heritage.

One day after a Sunday lunch when my friend Mary Rogers was visiting, we discussed what the bridesmaids would wear. She was to be one of the bridesmaids.

The Judge said, "Of course they will wear orange and black, the Princeton colors."

Mummy, not realizing he was teasing, protested: when he said, "I'll not pay for it otherwise," she burst into tears.

Meanwhile, I continued to attend balls, lunches and theater parties. I was immensely bored with the whole thing. The only activity that really interested me that year was a provisional training program at the Junior League, run by Clare Tousley of the Community Service Society. Eleanor

Roosevelt was among those who spoke to the young members about the National Recovery Administration and the conditions in the country that called for such drastic action by the government. I felt uplifted by the talk, as though I was back in college again, and I found Mrs. Roosevelt inspiring.

George Cole was pleased that the engagement had given him an excuse to leave Richmond and take a job in New York. He felt he finally had the opportunity to escape the clutches of his mother, a clinging and manipulative woman whom he didn't know how to manage. As difficult and dictatorial as my mother was, George's problem did seem worse. Our mutual trials and tribulations with our mothers created a bond between us.

The other bond was our physical attraction. George, more demonstrative than my parents, often told me he loved me, but he was clearly interested in sex. He introduced me to necking in the backseat of the family car under the cover of a thick lap rug. There was a glass partition between us and the chauffeur, who always looked straight ahead, no matter how much we giggled. We assumed he couldn't hear a thing, but he was probably perfectly aware of the goings-on behind his back.

Mummy had given me fairly explicit instructions about sex, but I did not have much experience with boys. I discovered she entirely omitted the fact that kissing and necking can be exciting and fun. George's mother never mentioned the subject, but on my first visit to Richmond a book on sex lay on the table next to my bed in the guest room. One night, when I was visiting again in Richmond, George kept me up late after his mother had gone to bed. He was a bit more aggressive than usual, and finally I found myself giving in to his advances. In my diary, I recorded that I "submitted to please him." I rationalized my actions to myself; thinking that since we were engaged, what we had done was not immoral.

I had been going along with the wedding planning, not thinking too much about it, but in February, just a few months before the wedding, something happened that forced me to look closely at where I was heading. Mummy suggested that George and I visit Granny Clark. Granny had a house in Augusta, Georgia, where she spent the winters after Grandpa Clark's death. We could spend some time together under Granny's watchful eye, my mother thought, and I could really "get to know George." It was a good idea in the abstract. The problem was that it worked. Granny was a very bright lady and interested in the world of ideas. During our visit, she and I spent hours talking about Smith and the courses I had taken. She loved to hear about my favorite course on the origin of the Great War. It was during these talks that I gradually realized what was amiss between George and me. He was a very sweet man, and he tried, but he was not interested in any intellectual discussion. All he could talk about was fox hunting in Virginia and fishing in Scotland. Neither Granny nor I were interested in those topics. After three weeks, I had discovered that my fiancé and I had next to nothing in common. What on earth, I found myself wondering, will we talk about after we were married? In my bedroom at night, I felt the walls closing in on me.

By the time we got back to Princeton, I knew I must tell Mummy that I had made a big mistake. I was not ready for marriage, for such a final commitment. The wedding must be postponed, and I wanted to go back to Smith.

But when I told Mummy she was appalled. "But I've made all the plans and ordered the invitations," she said. Though I tried to argue, Mummy was adamant. She may have been concerned about my youth earlier but now she would not back off. "All girls go through this kind of thing," Mummy said by way of reassurance, thinking all I had was the usual case of cold feet.

I knew it was more than that, but I was helpless in the face of my parents' determination. Mummy barged ahead. I did not know at that time that she was going through a traumatic period herself with Father, who had numerous love affairs and was engaging in a high profile affair with a well–known designer. Perhaps, I now think, Mummy felt overwhelmed by her own troubles and thought it was best for me to be married and away from home.

And, too, the wedding planning was a wonderful distraction for her. She enjoyed every minute and every aspect of the preparations, from the ceremony and reception to the clothes I would take on my honeymoon and the linens for my future home. In her office she had a bulletin board with plans pinned precisely and she ran the wedding like a military campaign. The Peacock Inn, a small hotel nearby, was reserved for the out–of–town bridesmaids and ushers. Rooms at the Princeton Inn were reserved for the Virginia delegation. Two upstairs bedrooms in our house were used to display the wedding presents on tables covered with white damask cloths.

I wrote 454 thank you notes, using a green book in which Mummy recorded the presents. As she unpacked one present from Richmond, she turned up her nose and wrote, "A horrible yellow vase." Without thinking I had become little more than an automaton. I wrote: "Dear Mrs._____, Thank you for the horrible yellow vase."

The wedding day came on May 19, 1934. I had a maid of honor and twelve bridesmaids who wore identical white dresses with small trains and a crimson panel down the back. George had twelve ushers in striped gray trousers, swallowtail morning coats, gray spats, and gloves. This was the *de rigueur* for that kind of wedding.

The Judge led me down the aisle of Trinity Church, Princeton, New Jersey, only too joyously. I walked beside him in a kind of daze, staring at George and the wedding party waiting for me at the altar, but not really seeing anything. My face was frozen in a smile because a smile was called for. I did not feel like a real person, like Anne Blair Clark, living a real occasion, stepping out into the rest of her life.

I felt like an actress in a play—a very bad play.

Chapter Four

I was only 19 years old when I married George, but I had already seen great changes in the world. Horse–drawn carriages had been overtaken by automobiles, corsets by brassieres, the long trailing skirts of my youth by sleek, body–skimming dresses that revealed a great deal of leg. In 1934 the telephone had become a common medium of communication for those who could afford it, and the radio was bringing the voice of the world directly into people's homes. Refrigerators had replaced ice boxes. The Great War had changed the United States from a relatively young, largely isolationist country into an increasingly formidable player—the Great Depression notwithstanding—on the world stage.

Some things, though, stayed the same. Women had the right to vote for 14 years, but it was still assumed by many of them that the one thing they wanted out of life and the role for which they were best suited, was to marry, have children, raise a family, and run a household. This was particularly true for women of my social class—we were never supposed to have to work for a living. Still, this outline of a life seemed spare. I felt somehow cheated, as though another part of life, a rich and important one—the life of the mind, of the intellect—had been denied to me. And for all my affection for George, I knew he hadn't tapped any deep well of love in me. Nevertheless, here I was; a young wife, with a husband I felt was little more than a boy; and my whole life spreading before me like a vast unbroken plain where the scenery was dull and never–changing.

I have always had a practical mind. Ever since Nanny

left, when confronted with a situation that makes me unhappy, that I know I can't alter, my way of dealing with it is to put my head down and forge ahead. Having married George Cole, I knew there was nothing I could do to change the path my life was set on. I was a married woman and I would have to make the best of it. "Who knows?" I said to myself. "Maybe I could even have fun."

George certainly wanted to have fun. Before the wedding, we talked about having children, but he wanted to wait two years before we'd start a family. That was fine with me. He must have divulged his plans to his brother–in–law, Bernard, because Bernard's wedding present to us was a twelve dozen Trojan condoms. But on our honeymoon in Scotland, George's plan quickly went "agley," as the Scots say.

One lovely afternoon, we climbed the steep hill to the moors for a picnic. After sandwiches and wine, we started to hug and kiss, buried in the heather. George murmured something about having forgotten the condoms.

Not long afterward, I came down with food poisoning, or so I thought. It was a logical assumption, since some Scots, who counted on their cool climate to keep food from spoiling, didn't rely on refrigeration. We made our way to London, where a Mr. Atkins, a physician from fashionable Harley Street, arrived at our hotel to examine me. He was dressed in a morning coat with tails and striped trousers, and carried a gray top hat in his hand. I asked him if he was on his way to the races—his costume was identical to one George had rented for a day of races at Ascot. In a tone doubtless reserved for uncultured Americans, he informed me he was on his way to his office. He asked me a few questions, but didn't examine me. Then he told George that I had appendicitis.
He took out a little book, poised a pencil above it, and announced that he could perform the operation on Tuesday.

"But my appendix was removed five years ago," I said.

Mr. Atkins beat a hasty retreat, but later we received a bill for five guineas, roughly $50.

Three weeks after our wedding, my mother–in–law, who liked to be called Mummy Hillie, arrived in London to join us for the social season. When George told her I was ill, she insisted we move in with her at the Hyde Park Hotel. So we moved.

I was too weak to go out, so my mother–in–law went to all the parties with her adored son as her escort. She felt like she was in heaven.

I recovered very slowly, but in early August I was well enough so we could set sail for New York on the Hamburg–American line. My ailment was diagnosed, ultimately, as colitis, but it had been masking an underlying condition. When I missed my period for the second month, I was quite sure I was pregnant. I broke the news to George on the boat. He looked at me and then blurted out, "What will we do with all those condoms?" Good Scot that I am, I suggested keeping them for future use, but he had a better idea. That night, we blew them up into balloons and floated them out the porthole.

I remember being terrified at the prospect of childbirth. My own mother's lurid descriptions of my birth came washing back over me as I contemplated all it entailed. Forty–eight hours of agony, she had called it.

Meanwhile I was gravely concerned about my mother. My father's infidelities had increased in frequency and openness. Returning from Europe, George and I joined my parents in Newport, where they had taken a "cottage" for the summer. And at long last, my mother began to confide in me because I was a "married woman." Father had been unfaithful to her from the second year of their marriage, she told me. Recently, she had hired a private detective to follow him. His findings had upset her deeply. She spent days shut up in her room in bed, crying. She seemed emotionally fragile, even unstable. I wondered, listening to her, how she could have put up with my father's faithlessness for so long. I was sure it was something I could never tolerate. Years later, though, I would learn firsthand not only the pain of a husband's infidelity, but the lengths to which a woman would go to live with it for the sake of family, appearances and stability—all at the cost of her own self–esteem.

One morning, the newspapers carried an article about a woman who had thrown herself out an eighteenth story window to her death in New York. She was my father's latest love. My Auntie Deedee called to warn me that I should keep the newspapers from my mother. But it was too late; she had read it. The article seemed to send her into despair. She became hysterical, threatening suicide herself. I phoned Auntie Deedee, who summoned a doctor. My mother, he determined, was in a need of serious psychiatric care, and she was eventually admitted to the Riggs sanitarium in Lenox, Massachusetts.

In spite of Mummy's illness, my married life started out well. I found a lovely furnished apartment at 96th street and Fifth Avenue, on the fringes of the prime Upper East Side neighborhood, for only $200 a month. The large, elegant living room was furnished in muted rose and blue velvet–covered chairs and sofas. Blue silk curtains framed the windows overlooking Central Park through which the afternoon sun poured in. A bedroom, dining room, kitchen, and a guest room rounded out the space.

George, who was good with figures, made out a budget for us, gave me a household allowance, and balanced my checkbook. Our expenses were well within our income of $10,000 a year, which was quite a good sum for the times.

Having never been allowed in the kitchen while growing up, I had no idea of how to cook or even how to shop for food. I hired a pleasant Swedish woman as cook–housekeeper for $75 a month. But when she wasn't there, I was helpless. My elderly cousin Mildred came to call one afternoon. I had to apologize for not being able to offer her tea, as it was the cook's day off.

"My dear," Cousin Mildred declared, "I'll show you how to make tea."

In addition to boiling water and brewing tea, I eventually learned how to heat things up after our cook had prepared them.

What made me happiest in these early days were the classes I attended at Barnard College. I saw the opportunity to continue the education I was forced to abandon at Smith.

I took the bus up Fifth Avenue every day, delighted to be learning again. Along with the courses, students were required to take some athletics. I went to my advisor and explained that I was pregnant.

"May I take swimming?" I asked. "I like that best."

"How can you do that when you're pregnant?"

"My doctor thinks it's all right."

"But we don't. When you're in a bathing suit the girls will notice that you're pregnant, and that won't do."

But my delight was short–lived. About six weeks into the semester, George woke up one night with severe stomach pain—appendicitis. After the operation, Mummy Hillie, who had come up, of course, to be by her son's side, announced that she had taken a suite in the Brazilian Court Hotel in Palm Beach where we should come for George to recuperate as soon as he was well enough to travel. I protested, not wanting to leave my classes. But Mummy Hillie would have none of it, calling college nonsense for a girl like me. "Your husband comes first," she declared.

We went to Florida.

Mummy Hillie was going strong now. On our return to New York, George was scheduled to start work at the Clark thread company in Newark. Being a stockbroker in 1934 was neither interesting nor lucrative, so George was hired as an intern at the thread company. His mother insisted he was not strong enough to make the commute from our 5th Avenue apartment. We must move to Newark, or at least further downtown in Manhattan. A friend of hers owned an apartment on Ninth Street, near the Hudson tubes. It would lengthen my commute to school from 45 minutes to nearly two hours.

No matter what I said to George or his mother, they seemed to consider the matter of the apartment settled. I dropped out of college for a second time. George and I moved into the dreary little apartment on Ninth Street, saving George all of 15 minutes on the Hudson tubes.

I didn't complain. I wonder now why I gave in on matters that were so important to me. But all I can say is that as a young wife, I hadn't learned how to speak up for myself, let alone how to stand my ground and make a fuss if necessary. Instead, I didn't allow myself to realize that I was unhappy, disappointed and, most of all, angry.

March 11, 1935, nine months and two weeks after George and I were married, I went into labor. George said, "As a friend of mine said, I just had time to remove my shoes."

Early in my pregnancy, Mummy had insisted that I see the fashionable Dr. Hildreth. Her friends said that he was the best obstetrician in New York. I was uneasy from the outset, since he insisted on a kind of general anesthesia—called "twilight sleep"—for the delivery. But Mummy pressed, and so when the labor began, I reported to the Harbor Hospital and Dr. Hildreth drugged me into a state of unconsciousness.

Marjory Blair Scott, weighing six pounds four ounces, and later named for my mother, arrived at 4:48 p.m.. I had never seen a new baby. Although she grew into a beautiful child, I was struck by how tiny she was. She did not look like my dolls. Somehow I had expected that she would.

Thanks to Dr. Hildreth, Marjory and I were toxic from the anesthetic for days. I nursed Marjory for six weeks, but George insisted that I stop, saying that nursing would ruin my figure.

George and I settled into family life. Our second child, George, weighing seven and a half pounds, was born July 9, 1937. The doctor had to use forceps to deliver him. I did not repeat the same mistake and was not given "twilight sleep." We named him George Cole Scott III—there must be a George Cole in each generation, my mother–in–law insisted.

In August 1939, the winds of war began to blow. Mummy had reconciled with father after her release from Riggs. They took a house on the Long Island shore, and we spent several weeks with them. Mummy listened endlessly to the radio and the reports of Hitler's movements in Europe. One night, George suggested that if we still wanted three children, we had better start thinking about having the third. So David was conceived to the sound of the guns of August and the marching feet in Europe heard on the radio in Mummy's room next door.

David Cameron Scott was born three weeks early on May 19, 1940, weighed six and a half pounds. He had a beautifully shaped head. Unfortunately, he developed eczema and had to live on goat's milk.

George had graduated from the Virginia Military Institute in the southern tradition, so it was only a matter of time that he would enlist to fight in World War II. He joined the 112th field artillery in Morristown, New Jersey in the summer of 1940. The following January, the 112th was activated with orders to report to Fort Bragg, North Carolina. Maisie Macy (the wife of George's friend Josh Macy, also an officer in the 112th) and I moved to Southern Pines, a town about 30 miles from Fort Bragg, to be near our husbands. We found that there were good private schools there, so I rented a little house on the edge of a golf course and enrolled Marjory and George in school.

When our husbands came home on the weekends, life was intensely social. George insisted that I go fox hunting with him. In the evenings, there were dinners and parties, and the alcohol flowed freely. George and I didn't fight about his heavy drinking, but our marriage was strained. We hadn't grown great a commonality of interests; not even our children could surmount the differences between us. Every Sunday, George had a tremendous hangover and spent most of the day on the living room couch, holding his head. I mentioned this to Maisie from time to time. She listened sympathetically, but she didn't know any more about alcoholism than I did.

After Pearl Harbor, living in a twilight world, we waited for news of the future. Finally, in May 1943, the 112th was deployed to the Pacific, to the island of Fiji. I wanted to take the children back to Peapack, New Jersey, to the house George and I had built in the 10 acre field we had bought from Grandpa Blair. But Mummy pressured me to come to Princeton, insisting the schools were better there.

As usual, I gave in, rented the house in Peapack and moved to a house within a block away from Mummy, who had come into her own running the Princeton Red Cross. War brought out the best in her. Within a couple of months of my move to Princeton, the Red Cross offered her the job of director of the eastern region, the organization's number three position. This formidable organizer had found a role, but at a price to me. Before Thanksgiving, Mummy moved to Washington. My school friends had moved away, so I spent the loneliest year of my life in Princeton.

This no doubt added to my sense of depression that year. I had expected to be doing a lot with my mother, but once she was gone, I was really left alone.

Eventually, I did find a job through the Red Cross, working as a nurse's aide at the Princeton hospital, helping to fill the void created by a shortage of nurses during wartime. The work was largely menial, not much above emptying bedpans—which I did a lot of—but it made me feel useful and I went to work every day full of enthusiasm. I wrote to my mother–in–law: "I love the work at the hospital. If it weren't for the children, I'd even work Thanksgiving and Christmas."

George had landed in Fiji from whence he sent long letters. "They describe sex here as bang–bang," he wrote and told me that he had danced with the chief's wife, who pointed out a portrait of a British officer and said her grandfather had eaten him. "All but the legs," she said, "they were too tough." They were, George wrote, encased in riding boots.

The distance between George, the children, and me began to grow. What saved us all in this difficult period, I believe, was my decision to become involved in business, inn keeping, in fact.

Actually, it was not a decision so much as an impulse. I was sitting with the children one early spring morning in 1944 in Peapack, reading their favorite book, *The Little Engine That Could,* when the telephone on the library table rang. It was Hans Falkner, an Austrian ski instructor that I had met in Canada the year before on a skiing trip to Mont Tremblant, Quebec, with my friend Marjo Dewey and her husband. We had had a wonderful time, taking skiing lessons and picnicking at the top of the mountain. Hans's voice brought back the memories of the fir trees covered with snow, looking like pyramids of diamonds glistening in the afternoon sun. We had all fallen in love with the charming resort. Each evening, after a day of skiing in the crystalline air, we had gathered in the bar before dinner to talk about the resort's owner, whom we didn't like and to fantasize about owning a ski lodge of our own. Now, Hans was calling to tell me our fantasy could become a reality.

Hans had found a lodge for sale near St. Sauveur, another ski town closer to Montreal. He hoped the Deweys and I might seriously consider buying it and make him the ski instructor there. Almost on a whim, Bud Dewey and I made the trip north to scout out the possibility. We took the night train to Montreal and then transferred to the Laurentian local train. Each car of the train, warmed by a pot–bellied stove, was filled with skiers.

Hans met us at the railroad station in Piedmont. A sleigh and driver took us up toward the mountain. St. Sauveur was enchanting; we passed little cottages in rainbow hues of pale blue, pink, red and yellow as the sleigh creaked up the snowy road. The view from the mountain was breathtaking. At the top, I could see Mont Royale, 40 miles to the south in Montreal. The main house on the property hugged the hillside and was made of logs. It was built by Josephine Hartford, the A&P heiress. Next to it was the biggest woodpile I had ever seen, nearly as high as the house.

We opened the front door, and the scent of polished logs wafted over us. Inside, the song "Rum and Coca–Cola" was playing on a record player in the living room. Several workmen, clad in blue jeans and plaid work shirts, were shuffling on the floor in time to the music, pieces of lambskin tied loosely over their shoes. They were polishing the wood floors. A fire was burning in the whitewashed fireplace in the corner of the main room. The chandelier in the dining room was made of crossed skis adorned with lights. Deerskins hung on the walls and bearskins covered the floor. The overall effect was warm and romantic. Bud and I were enthralled.

Within weeks, the Deweys, two other couples and I – with George's approval and acquiescence via the mail – had pooled our resources and bought Mont Gabriel, 500 acres, and a trout stream for $30,000 Canadian. The other two couples were chiefly investors. Marjo and I planned to run the place. That December, on Christmas day, we opened our own ski resort, one of only a handful in North America at the time.

We hired a cast of characters to staff it. Tommy Nuthall, the manager, looked like a toby jug, with a round tummy and a red nose. But he was a whiz at hotel management. He spent most of the day in his tiny back office, preparing room charts, bills for the guests and paying our accounts. When off duty, he entertained guests in the bar, where Jerry, the bartender, a genial redheaded Irishman, presided for as long as there was guest awake to request a drink or some companionship.

We enjoyed entertaining our guests after dinner. Many an evening we rolled up the rugs, and George, the butler, was given disk jockey duty, loading waltzes and polkas onto the old record player. To get the dancing started, Hans would beckon to me and we would step out in time to a waltz. I waltzed for miles that winter.

My chief responsibility was the day shift. I rose early in the morning to plan meals with Hilda, the chef. I talked to the chambermaids, Martha and Sirka, to let them know about guest arrivals and departures. I discussed the table arrangement with George and conferred with Hans about the ski trails and his classes. And I talked to Tommy about finances.

From the shy and diffident girl and young woman I had been, I blossomed into a fairly knowledgeable businesswoman, learning to operate with diplomacy, tact, and political skill. As an innkeeper, I had to learn to cajole and persuade. When the water pump repeatedly broke down and could not be replaced, I charmed a guest into helping us repair it. To avoid complaints, I would show guests initially into one room, and then show them another, so that they could choose the "better" room, which was in fact the room actually booked for them.

Mont Gabriel lost $13,000 in that first year—actually not too great a loss for a startup business. If we could keep it going, we expected we could even make some money or at least break even, in our second season. Despite the financial loss, Mont Gabriel was decidedly a *succès d'estime*. It was the "in" place of the year. *Vogue* magazine, among many others, scheduled a photo shoot on our premises with the leading model of the season, Jessica Barkentin. A young photographer named Richard Avedon was doing the shoot; he was just coming into his own. Jessica was a beautiful girl who had been featured on 23 magazine covers in the previous year. As it happened, my brother Bill was visiting Mont Gabriel when she arrived. They met and fell madly in love. But after a brief relationship, they went their separate ways.

Forty years later, in the 1980s, after Bill's wife Elly died, Bill looked up Jessica, who had divorced her husband, in the New York phone book. He called and left a message on her answering machine, saying he would like to see her again but failed to leave his own number. Jessica, fortunately, was a smart girl, and remembered that my brother Blair at CBS news was Bill's brother. She called him and said, "Please tell Bill I don't want to wait another 40 years to see him." She and Bill met again and lived happily together for many years.

Running an inn offered an opportunity to view the whole range of human behavior. Some romances were born and others died at Mont Gabriel. Some ladies chased the gentlemen, and some gentlemen chased the ladies. The locals had a saying: "There's no sex on the mountain." Don't believe it!

Mont Gabriel did well enough so that we decided to stay open for a short summer season with a smaller staff. One of our guests was Dr. Lin Yutan, the author of *The*

Importance Of Living, a very influential book in the 1940s. That summer Dr. Lin was working on a project to reduce the 4,000 characters of the Chinese language to a number that could fit a typewriter keyboard. One day, he said to Tommy Nuthall, "The two ladies here, Mrs. Dewey and Mrs. Scott, are charming. But I have trouble telling them apart. The only way I can differentiate between them is that Mrs. Scott is pinker."

It was amusing to hear guests' assessments of us. I was highly entertained by the comments of one French Canadian lady who came to ski for a day with the man who would turn out to be Marjo's second husband after her divorce from Bud.

"This is a wonderful place," Bob Graff said to his companion. "Who owns it?"

His date was overheard responding, "Two frosty ladies from New York."

For the first time in my life, I thought of myself as successful. I was accomplishing something real and concrete and growing in ways I never anticipated. There was clearly something of my mother in me, for she, too, had been immensely successful in her work with the Red Cross. The executive in us, freed to emerge, had flourished.

Nevertheless, the habit of tradition died hard. I fully expected that when George returned from the war, I would resume my life as a married lady, running a home and overseeing a family, and leaving the business end of things to my husband. George had enthusiastically approved the decision to invest in Mont Gabriel, seeing it as an opportunity to create an independent source of income that would free him to leave the thread company. Before the war, he had thought of buying a farm.

In 1945, George had been away, "somewhere in the Pacific," for three years. He had been prohibited from telling me much of what was happening to him in his letters. While in Canada, I was able to hear news of the European front and in New Jersey, all the papers, even the *New York Times*, focused on the war in Europe. As a result, I had only the sketchiest knowledge of George's war. When he finally came home in July, 1945, I had no concept of his experiences.

George telephoned from California to say that he would be arriving in New York the following day. I should meet him there, he said, at a friend's apartment.

I told Father about George's return. "That's going to be a very romantic meeting," Father said and suggested that I buy a sexy black nightgown for the occasion. So I did.

George and I did have a romantic few days. He was so thin, at six feet tall, he weighed only 125 pounds. He was very nearly emaciated. I tried to draw him out, to get him to talk about the war. But he couldn't, or wouldn't. And he never could, even years later. Of course, this is not unusual. Our grandson Kenny doesn't speak of his experiences after being deployed to Iraq and Afghanistan. It's always hard.

After his discharge, we drove to Canada in my small gray car. Marjory and George remembered their father, but David was hiding somewhere. We finally found him on the roof. I remember him asking me only a few days before: "What's a father?"

We all had enormous adjustments to make—the children to their father, George to civilian life, the two of us to a new way of life and the business of running a hotel. George had the hardest part of it and he was drinking most of every day. He considered Mont Gabriel his private domain, ignoring the fact that there were other partners. When Marjo came up, he refused to discuss the inn's future or past with her. She was upset. "I feel as if he's telling me to go back and play with my dolls, Anne," she told me. "He doesn't want to hear any of my suggestions." George didn't want any suggestions from me either.

Marjo sent her financial advisor, Jackson Martindell, to Mont Gabriel to evaluate the situation. After a couple of days of interviewing the staff and me, he reported to Marjo that he believed the place was a good investment, but that the partnership could not survive. Marjo offered to buy us out. It seemed to me the sensible thing to do, since Marjo had the money to purchase our share and since George had neither the know–how nor the funds to manage a sole ownership. But George's emotional investment in the place was huge. He had dreamed about it during the war. He simply couldn't bear to give it up. In the end, he bought out all the other partners, investing far more than we could afford.

It was a disastrous decision, like the ones that followed. George hired a manager to run the resort and went back to work at the Clark Thread Company. We bought a charming townhouse on Mountain street in Montreal and went up to Mont Gabriel on weekends. But his alcoholism and the strain in our marriage only increased.

We went on this way for two more years. We had no idea about marriage counseling—very few people did at the time. But we realized that our relationship was deteriorating. We discussed separation and divorce. Finally, on November 26, 1947, George formally asked me for a divorce. He drew up a tentative separation agreement. My mother had seen this coming and she recommended her own divorce attorney. He in turn recommended we see a psychiatrist. After several sessions with George, the psychiatrist told me that George's problems stemmed from his childhood and that it was not the war that caused his alcoholism. But neither the psychiatrist nor anyone else ever suggested Alcoholics Anonymous. That organization had been founded in 1935, but we didn't even know it existed.

After months of psychotherapy, George and I decided to proceed with the divorce. I got custody of the children. They would visit George for half the summer and either

Christmas or Easter holidays. George set up a fund to pay
for the children's education. George got Mont Gabriel, which
he was eventually forced to sell, having never realized a profit
from it. Only a few years after he sold it, the new owner sold it
again for a handsome profit at $10 million. Today, it is worth
much, much more than that.

After the marriage was over, I sometimes thought of
our divorce as a tragedy that might have been avoided with
proper counseling. At other times, it seemed to me that the
real mistake was the marriage itself. George was as much of a
victim as I of our parents' desire for a "suitable marriage."

George eventually remarried, moved to Richmond,
started a successful business and had the busy social life he
and his new wife deemed important. He remained close to
Marjory, but was more distant with George and David, who
had not known him as well. I always thought of him as an
honorable man who had been caught in a situation he was
unable to resolve. Much later, when he was terminally ill, I
told him how badly I had felt for him, and he was kind and
forgiving.

As a girl, I had unwittingly and unwillingly entered a
gilded cage, and it finally broke open in 1948, after almost
15 years. I felt free, but I didn't know what the future would
hold. I was very unrealistic about money. Granny Clark had
left me a small amount when she died. But I had no real idea
of what it would cost me to live on my own. I thought my
mother would help, but in fact, she couldn't, as she too was
divorced and receiving no alimony. My father had remarried.
He had an enormous income from his own father's trust,
which my brothers and I would divide upon his death. But my
father actually resented this and was in no mood to help any
of his children.

I did not realize it, but my financial position was
precarious. I was not specifically trained for any occupation
and I had three young children to raise.

Chapter Five

Some call it the accuracy of chance, but my second marriage was really a series of well–timed circumstances. First came an acquaintanceship; then a sense of panic at finding myself alone, with limited resources and three children to raise; and a man's interest at just the right time.

Jackson Martindell was Marjo Dewey's investment counselor, the one who came up to Mont Gabriel to look at our books. He came to offer financial advice and to help resolve the conflict between George and Marjo regarding Mont Gabriel. He was a striking man, but if anyone had told me that I would soon be married to him, I would have thought such an idea was absurd. After all, I was a married woman and he appeared to be courting Marjo. One summer, Marjo took me to his house in Bernardsville to play tennis. He lived in an old, rambling, comfortable house surrounded by acres of lawn and lovely gardens. On that occasion, I found Jackson handsome, intelligent, warm, and jolly.

By 1948, my situation had changed completely. In the middle of my divorce from George, I was confused and more than frightened—I was very nearly in a panic over my situation. I didn't know how I would manage on my own. By then, too, Marjo had definitely turned Jackson down, and slowly—I don't even know exactly when or how it happened —he began to take an interest in me.

Maybe it was largely my circumstances, or the force of his personality, or his elaborate tales, but I did return his interest. He seemed in many ways an ideal prospect for a husband. I found him physically attractive. He was fairly tall, dark haired, with piercing hazel eyes. When I visited him again at his own house, he struck me as a warm and loving father to his three children by his first marriage. He was funny and entertaining, loved games, and loved to play with both his children and mine. There never seemed to be a dull moment when Jackson was around.

He dazzled me with his tall tales of growing up in the Southwest and later working on Wall Street. He'd been born in Abilene, Texas, the son of an official with the Santa Fe Railroad who was in charge of building the tracks across West Texas to New Mexico. When Jackson was eight or nine years old, his father bought some land in New Mexico's Sangre de Cristo Mountains and built a house there. It was wild country in those days, home to many lawless desperadoes.

Jackson's father was often away laying railroad tracks, so the boy and his mother were home alone a great deal of the time. Jackson was taught how to shoot a gun; he was trained to know that if anyone came down the road to the house, he was to go to the upstairs window and shoot if his mother gave the signal. One day, when he was about 10 years old, a man rode up and called out, asking if anyone was home. Jackson, watching from the window, thought he saw a man draw his pistol. He fired—and the man fell from his horse, dead.

The next day, the Marshall from the nearby town of Raton came to see Jackson's parents. The adults struck a deal—if Jackson left New Mexico, he would not be prosecuted. So he was sent to live with his aunt and uncle at Crawford Place, the family ranch near Houston. Today, George W. Bush's Crawford Ranch occupies a piece of this former property. Jackson lived there for six years, exiled from his parents. Eventually, he joined his parents in Denver, attended the University of Colorado, dropped out to enlist in the army, went overseas in the Great War; and served as a motorcycle messenger. Then he went back to Boulder to finish college and eventually made his way to New York to study journalism at Columbia. But rather than pursue that career, he ended up with a Wall Street investment firm and found his niche, eventually setting up his own company. For a time, he advised the Franklin Roosevelts on their finances, a connection that led to a brief interest in politics. In 1935, he raised funds and campaigned for Alf Landon. But when Landon lost the presidential election in a landslide, Jackson gave up on politics.

I've always believed the shooting episode that led to Jackson's exile scarred him for life, and he later wrote privately that it distorted his perception of people. He often felt that everyone regarded him with hostility. I have no doubt this contributed to the emotional instability that gradually revealed itself to me after we were married. Over the years, I came to think of Jackson like the little girl in the nursery rhyme with the curl in the middle of her forehead. When he was good, he was very, very good; but when he was bad, he was horrid.

Early in our relationship, Jackson was still showing me his very best side. That summer of 1948, he was very, very good. He was openly affectionate. Warm affection freely given was something I had never known, except from Nanny and Mademoiselle Figuet. I found it enormously appealing.

My mother met Jackson that summer he was courting me. Since my divorce, she had tried to introduce me to a number of men she considered suitable. They were men like the impecunious heir to the Putnam publishing fortune, who offered to take the children and me sailing if I would charter the boat. Then, though he claimed to be an expert sailor, he made an error in judgment that ripped the sail—and he expected me to mend the tear before he would return the boat! Not surprisingly, the children dubbed him "Put–Put." I found him unpleasant and possibly sadistic. Later, he married a school friend of mine and then disappeared with most of her money.

My mother never said she disliked Jackson, but she actively encouraged any other man who had any interest in me. Yet when the crunch came, her rigid sense of propriety once again won out over her sense of my best interests. When I talked to an Episcopal minister about marrying Jackson, he advised that the church expected anyone to wait a year after a divorce before remarrying. I thought this was sensible advice and told Mummy I had decided to wait until a full year had passed before deciding whether to marry Jackson. She was alarmed.

"You can't do that," she exclaimed. "Obviously you're going to continue seeing Jackson, and all my friends will talk!"

I was puzzled. It seemed that once again my mother was pushing me into a marriage, this time to a man whom I was certain she disliked. Appearances seemed more important to her than the children's happiness or mine. Looking back, I can't help wondering why I did accept Jackson's proposal. Perhaps if I had waited, I might not have married him.

*   *   *   *   *

I became Mrs. Jackson Martindell on August 12, 1948, in a ceremony at the Congregational Church in Chatham, Massachusetts. My son George was the best man and holder of the ring. Soon after, at Jackson's urging, I used $25,000 of my legacy from Granny Clark to buy the house at 117 Library Place in Princeton from my father, the same house where I had lived as a child. Jackson believed it was a good move for the children's sake, that it represented stability and continuity, and the logic of his argument convinced me. I didn't realize, at the time, how the ghosts of my childhood still lingered there and how they would come out, in time, to remind me how unhappy my family had been in this house.

In the beginning Jackson tried hard to be a good husband and father. He went to services at Trinity Church and passed the plate as if he were a pillar of the community —even though he hadn't gone to church in years. Everything he did was geared toward what he believed would be good for the children—or at least so he said. He was fond of young George, and played games with him and showed him a good time. He worked to instill good work habits in the boy. And he was good with my littlest son, David, too. But Marjory never liked him. She was thirteen by then, an age at which she no doubt would have disliked any stepfather, any man who came into the picture and displaced her real father. She missed her friends in Montreal, too, and placed the blame for having to leave them on this new man in our lives. Before the wedding, Marjory had told me she thought I was making a mistake; it was brave of her.

Two years after our wedding, I became pregnant. Marjory by then was off to school at St. Timothy's, at Mummy's insistence, and George, at his father's direction, was attending boarding school in Virginia. David, now nine, was the only one at home, and he was very watchful and protective of me during my pregnancy. One day, Jackson took the three of us to an ice skating show at Baker Rink. It became clear that he was very taken with the young woman who was the principal skater. Jackson raved on and on about her at dinner, mostly to tease. Finally, David, my loyal little boy became indignant. "She's nice," he said with as much defiance as he could muster, "but not as nice as my mother."

One Sunday morning late in my pregnancy, I heard a tap on my bedroom door. When I called "Come in," David entered carrying a breakfast tray with an egg, toast, tea, and orange juice. He had prepared it all by himself.

Roger Clark Martindell was born on May 12, 1950. He

weighed in at nine pounds four ounces and was blessed with strong lung power. I hired a nurse to come home from the hospital, Miss Smythe, to care for him, and she stayed with us, on and off, for two years. Over this period, Jackson became increasingly domineering. He bullied me constantly. I often gave in for the sake of peace.

Though he could be affectionate and demonstrative, Jackson just as easily could turn hard, demanding, and very tough on the children. Essentially a loner at heart, he viewed the world as if it were arrayed against him. Like many loners, he liked animals better than people. We had a tricolor collie, called Jugger, who became the apple of Jackson's eye. One year, when Roger was two, Jackson was asked to do a management audit of Whitman College in Walla Walla, Washington, and our family was invited to spend a month on the campus that summer. We took Jugger along, stopping in Denver to visit with Jackson's parents.

When we boarded our flight from Denver to Walla Walla, Jackson was called to the back of the plane where an airline official told him that our dog could not be accommodated on the flight and would have to follow us to Washington State the next day. Jackson was infuriated. He stamped up the aisle, saying in a loud voice: "We're getting off. I was promised that our dog would always be with us. I won't leave him on the tarmac in a cage."

We all trooped off the plane behind Jackson—Roger, fifteen year–old Marjory, the nurse, and I. But when I got to the bottom of the steps, I stopped. "I can't do this to Roger," I said. "I'm going on."

"All right, you go ahead," Jackson said dismissively. "I'll follow tomorrow."

We all trooped back onto the plane, poor Marjory scarlet from embarrassment, and took off for Walla Walla. Jackson didn't show up until late the next night with Jugger.

The happiest times of my married life with Jackson
were the summers we spent at our house in the Adirondacks.
We discovered the region in 1956, while visiting friends in
Keene Valley. Jackson loved it; it was wild and beautiful and
reminded him of the West. We rented a dark, old–fashioned
cottage beside the Ausable River. Jackson was determined
to buy some land. Every day he'd go out with a real estate
agent looking for property. It rained a lot that year, but we
all came to love the area. When the clouds lifted, we could
see the mountains, which looked oddly familiar to me. Then,
one day, someone mentioned that Mlle. Figuet was back from
Europe, and everything fell into place. All those years when
I was growing up, my old teacher had sent postcards and
balsam pillows from the Adirondacks to the sad little girl she
had cared for back in Bernardsville. I had looked at these
mountains for years.

When I went to see Mademoiselle Figuet in her house,
where she had spent every summer for 35 years, she told me
she had thought of me often. "I felt so sorry for you," she
said. "No one seemed to care about you." We became fast
friends. I would visit her often after that, and she even taught
Roger a little French.

Meanwhile, Jackson had purchased a parcel of
land consisting of 65 acres; on it stood an old ramshackle
farmhouse. We fixed it up, creating a reflecting pool at the
back and building a glassed–in room that overlooked it, and
we moved in during the summer of 1957. It was wonderful
there. The older children spent summers climbing the nearby
peaks—there were 46 that rose more than 4,000 feet. Jackson,
meanwhile, continued to purchase land, often at tax sales; in
the end, he acquired about 4,000 acres.

The problem was that in the mountains, Jackson tended
to think of himself rather like Louis XIV. *"L'etat c'est moi,"*
seemed to be his motto. When the road past our house was

rerouted, the very bright streetlight that had lit it was left in place—right in front of our bedroom window. Jackson asked the town fathers if he could move the light. He even offered to pay for its removal. They said no, because the neighbors liked having the light where it was. They thought that was the end of the matter. They didn't know Jackson.

Night after night, Jackson took to sitting on the front porch, his shotgun across his lap. As soon as the light went on, he shot out the bulb. It was replaced; he shot it out again. After a time, he went back to the town fathers and declared that if the light were moved, whoever was shooting out the bulb might stop. The light was finally moved.

Jackson loved his small bulldozer, using it to push the earth around. He had dug the hole for the pool behind our house, for instance. Around 1965, he got the idea to build a pond for the village on some land he owned at the town's edge where there was a stream and a beaver dam. He announced his plans to me and went off, day after day, happily pushing mud around to create a pond.

Unfortunately, Jackson had failed to read the regulations of the Adirondack Park Agency that stated that one needed a permit in order to alter a stream bed. Jackson insisted this did not apply to him, as he owned the land on both sides of the stream, as this was the Texas tradition. But park officials stood firm; it was the State of New York, not Jackson Martindell, which owned the streambed, they informed him. They urged him to apply for a permit. But Jackson would have none of it. He came home fuming.

"I'm not going to ask any bureaucrat for permission to do anything on my own land," he announced.

I offered to go and get the permit for him, as did two friends, but Jackson rejected the idea. He went on bulldozing, until one day a state trooper came by with a summons, ordering him to appear in court at the county seat of

Elizabethtown and to cease and desist from working on the stream in the meantime.

Jackson hired a lawyer and went off to court, furious. Though Jackson argued that as owner he had the right to decide what to do with his land, the judge wasn't buying it. He levied a hefty fine on Jackson. On the way home, I rather tactlessly spoke up. "The judge had a point," I said. Jackson turned white with anger. "Tomorrow I leave this place and I'm never coming back," he said. And that is just what he did. He never returned to our Adirondack house. His clothes hung in the closet, untouched, for twenty years, until I sold the house in 1987.

When Roger was in second grade, the head of his school, Mary Mason, called me in for a conference. Roger was having some difficulties in school; he was probably hyperactive and easily distracted. Mary suggested that we should send him to the North Country School, a school in the Adirondacks where we had been planning to send Roger much later. But Mary thought he should go now. The next fall, I drove Roger up to the North Country School in our red pickup truck. "Is it too late for me to change my mind?" he asked, eyeing the school warily. He has only just realized that I wouldn't be staying with at this new school.

Sending him there was one of the best decisions we ever made. The North Country School was run by Walter and Leo Clark, progressive educators who followed the philosophy of John Dewey. Their school treated children as individuals, encouraging the children to express themselves and they listened attentively to what the children had to say. The school stressed awareness of the environment and the way the natural world and human beings fit together. The children had jobs around the farm and school—Roger was assigned to care for the pigs ("I'm the pig man," he wrote home to me exuberantly) while others gathered eggs or plucked chickens.

They worked in the gardens growing organic vegetables and took turns milling the grain to make bread. They chopped trees, climbed mountains on skis, and slept in the woods on cold winter nights. Their training concentrated less on learning specific skills and more on how to take on jobs, even unpleasant ones, and see them through to a satisfactory conclusion. It was a process designed to build the kind of confidence that would last a lifetime.

I was deeply impressed by the school. Its academic standards were high, and the academic subjects were taught in novel ways. Mathematics, for instance, was related to practical problems, such as measuring the classroom. The children wrote and performed their own plays. Music, painting, and crafts were considered important and treated with respect.

From the Clarks, I learned an entirely new way of looking at children, at education, and even at life. My earlier life had been conventional, privileged and narrow, and my parents had stressed appearances above substance. But at North Country, the Clarks offered a life of diversity, of communion with the earth, of oneness with others. After seeing how different life can be from the way it was for me as I grew up, I would never be quite the same.

In October 1953, Father sent me a letter. Life had changed greatly for him. His last appointment had been as Chief Judge of the Allied Courts in Germany to hear cases involving U.S. citizens. He had ruled that some G.I.s who had broken German laws should be punished for their crimes. James Conant, the former President of Harvard who was the U.S. High Commissioner in Germany, disagreed with Father's ruling. He and Father had several arguments. One concerned the charge that the State Department was using recording devices on its telephones but did not disclose this fact. Father also claimed that Conant, who had overruled a number of Father's decisions, was interfering with the court.

There's no doubt that the court's work had narrowed by this time and a number of judges had returned to the United States. But Father felt he still had many important cases to hear and he wanted to remain in Germany to complete them. Nevertheless, he was ordered to vacate his job and his home in Frankfurt. Then, when he and his second wife, Sonia, left town for a vacation in the Canary Islands, Conant cabled the Secretary of State to say he wanted Father recalled to Washington immediately and had his diplomatic passport cancelled. Sonia had to go to Germany alone to retrieve their belongings.

It was an undignified end to a distinguished career, and it angered Father greatly. I could empathize, because even though he was often wrong and outrageous on a personal level, Father was usually right professionally. His opinions were highly regarded, by everyone from Bethuel Webster, once President of the New York Bar Association, to Justice William O. Douglas of the Supreme Court.

Early one morning in October 1957, my brother Blair telephoned. He had had a cable from Sonia, from Sri Lanka, where she and Father had been vacationing.

"How are they?" I asked innocently.

"Father died of a heart attack," Blair said. Father was 67.

I must have turned white as a sheet from shock. Yet I could not say the expected: I could not speak of grief. It seemed more like relief.

The ceremonies that followed Father's death would have made him proud. There were essentially three funerals: a service at Madison Avenue Presbyterian Church in New York, where Grandpa Clark had been an elder; a second service in the Princeton University Chapel; and finally a burial service at Arlington National Cemetery, where Father was given all the honor due a colonel in the armed forces.

Six black cavalry horses went before the coffin. A bugler played "Taps." The slow, sad notes filled the autumn air. The flag that draped the coffin was folded and presented to Sonia, his wife. I wept for what might have been.

*　*　*　*　*

After Father's death, Jackson made a strange remark. "Well, now that you will inherit your grandfather's trust, that's the end of our marriage." I felt betrayed by him and yet, he was right. But it wasn't just the money. As his infidelities continued, I didn't lean on him as much and we grew apart. Our marriage went on for another decade because I was afraid to be on my own. After 40 years of conformity, my life was soon to begin to take more surprising and dramatic turns.

Chapter Six

Late in the summer of 1964, just before Roger's last year at North Country School in Lake Placid, NY, Mary Mason invited me to tea. Mary ran a school for young children in Princeton. We talked about her recent trip to England. While there, she had met Sir James Pitman, whose family had invented shorthand. She told me that he had introduced her to a remarkable way of teaching reading with an alphabet he had invented, the "Initial Teaching Alphabet." It was based on the fact that the English language, while using only 26 letters, actually had 44 different sounds. The ITA alphabet thus consisted of 44 symbols, to represent all these different sounds. I was fascinated by everything Mary was telling me, but as I munched on a cucumber sandwich, I wondered why she was telling me all this.

Then Mary dropped a bombshell on me.

"Anne," she said, fixing her eyes on me with a determined look, "I want you to teach reading at my school using this method and I want you to start in September."

I was flabbergasted. "But I have no experience," I protested, "and no degrees!"

Mary smiled. "That's just why I want you," she said. "You have no preconceived ideas. I think you'd be perfect to teach this."

I didn't know what to think. I was flattered, but amazed that Mary would want someone like me. The thought of trying this new endeavor was exciting, but terrifying at the same time. I asked Mary to give me some time to think about it and to talk to Jackson, although I knew that Jackson probably wouldn't object unless my work interfered with his travel plans.

I talked to Mary again about the job and finally agreed to give it a try. I probably never would have undertaken this prior to my experience with North Country School. But having seen the wonders worked there, I felt inspired to contribute to the world of learning if I could.

To start with, Mary gave me very bright four–year–old children, my favorite age group. Children of this age still think any grown–up is God, and they're wonderfully spontaneous and curious. They hug your knees and are charmingly affectionate. I introduced the symbols with games, much as Mademoiselle Figuet had done with me many years ago, and then I got out of the way. My pupils not only survived my first year of teaching, they also learned to read and write very well.

The following summer I accompanied Mary to Great Britain and Scotland to attend a teaching conference and to visit schools that were teaching the ITA method. The conference was in Dundee, and I found the whole town redolent of the marmalade for which it was famous. Mary and I observed a classroom of 53 elementary students taught by one teacher. She had organized the bright ones to teach the slower ones, and she would personally teach only the children who were having the most difficulty. Every child was busy and seemed happy.

Later on that same trip, I traveled by myself through the British Isles and visited other schools. One day, I drove up in my rented car to visit a small school in a poor village in the mining district of Southern Wales. One of the teachers had made a man–sized rabbit out of cardboard. Using the ITA alphabet, she wrote tales of the rabbit's adventures. I loved the idea and decided to take it home with me. I was so entranced with the school that I stayed until lunch hour. The teachers invited me to join them for the meal. It consisted of boiled potatoes, salt, a little butter, and tea. In a mining town, that was a feast.

I returned home enthusiastic about teaching and threw myself into my work. I taught at Mary Mason's school for five years and it was a great source of strength during that time.

The sense of purpose I found in teaching was a good distraction from life with Jackson, which continued along its rather chaotic course. Jackson would show us all a good time when he was in a good mood, but he remained dictatorial and unpredictable. Over the years, however, I learned slowly to stand up to him.

Jackson was difficult and mercurial in his relationships with the children, even our own son, Roger. In 1966, Jackson and I were invited to Yugoslavia by a famous sculptor, Anton Augustincic, who had been Yugoslavia's minister for culture. We had met him several times on previous trips; now he wanted us to see Brioni, an island off the Dalmatian coast, and meet his boyhood friend, Yugoslav leader Marshal Tito, who maintained a summer residence there.

We took 16 year old Roger along with us and flew to Zagreb, then drove along winding mountain roads to Split, on the coast, in Augustincic's car, where a military boat met us and took us across the blue–green Adriatic to Brioni. We were put up in the official guesthouse, which, though small, was luxurious and elegant, furnished with brocade–covered French pieces and fine Oriental rugs. It also boasted a fully–stocked bar, which caused Jackson to comment that the leaders of the Communist countries appeared to live and drink very well.

Tito was due to arrive in a few days. Meanwhile, we swam in the clear water off a sandy beach during the day, while Roger played soccer with the young soldiers in the military guard. In the evening, we joined Augustincic and a number of high government officials on holiday in the main building for dinner, after which Jackson and the other men played chess, a game Jackson loved. He was a very good chess player.

After a few days, a professor who was with us informed us that the commander of the military guard did not want his soldiers fraternizing with an American, even a teenage boy on holiday with his parents. So Roger was cut off from his daytime activity, and we made plans to send him to Florence ahead of us. Tito was due to arrive the next day, and Jackson and I were invited to lunch with him.

So the next day, we sent Roger off to Florence and then climbed into an old-fashioned Victoria carriage pulled by a white horse—automobiles were not allowed on the island— and went off to the President's residence, a stucco villa with a red roof known as the "White Palace" over a mile away. Tito greeted us in the wood-paneled hall, where we signed the guest book, writing our names beneath those of Adlai Stevenson, Elizabeth Taylor, Queen Elizabeth, Ho Chi Minh, Nehru, Nasser, and many others.

Over lunch, Tito chatted about his fondness for American Western movies, which reminded him of what life had been like in Yugoslavia in the early 20th century. Jackson gave Tito a handsome wristwatch. Then I gave him my gift, a paperback copy of one of my favorite books, *The Silent Language*, by Richard Hall, about the way different cultures perceive time and space. He then launched into a story about an official trip he had taken to Brazil:

They flew over Brasilia, and as Tito told the story, "We circled, and we circled, and we circled. I sent for the pilot and asked, "Why are we not landing?" The pilot told me he had instructions to keep us in the air as the President of Brazil was not yet dressed. "I said to the pilot, you go down!" Tito illustrated, gesturing with his finger a downward circle, and continued, "The President, after we landed ran toward the steps of the airplane, still tying his tie!" Tito went on to tell us that he was escorted to the government guest house and informed that the official dinner in his honor would be held at 8 o'clock in the building next door. Tito continued the story.

"I dressed in my uniform, put on my medals, and walked to the building next door at eight. I was trained in the German Army to be punctual. When I arrived for the dinner at 8, no one was there, not even the chef and his staff who were to prepare the dinner." Tito paused for dramatic effect. "I will never, never go to Brasilia again!"

After lunch he showed us around his private zoo and took us to his own personal vineyard on the nearby island of Vanga. He was quite unassuming and a very good storyteller. It was a fascinating visit with a major figure in 20th century European history. But concern about Roger lingered.

On the following day, we took the Orient Express to Trieste. I was expecting spies, romance and good food. Instead, there was not only no food at all to be had, but also no water, and worst of all, no toilets. We hadn't thought to bring along something to eat. Then we sat for hours at the border with Italy while Italian police searched the train for drugs.

Twenty–four hours after leaving Brioni, we limped into Trieste. Jackson was fit to be tied. "I've had enough. We're getting off," he declared, announcing that we would fly to Rome and then directly home. I was appalled. "What about Roger?" I demanded. He was waiting for us in Florence. If we left him there, he wouldn't know what to do, what had become of us. Jackson was unmoved.

"It'll be good for him to be on his own," he declared. "I spent a lot of time alone. He has his ticket and passport. He'll figure out how to get home."

I couldn't argue him out of it. Nor could I do anything myself. I had very little cash with me and I knew Jackson wouldn't give me any to go to Florence. Suddenly, it dawned on me that he had probably planned this all along, from the moment we had left the States. Cry, argue, plead as I would, he wouldn't budge. Roger told me later, that he'd slept in the train station the first night, and for four days, he met every train coming into the Florence station.

Meanwhile, although I was almost entirely unaware of it, another passion was forming in my life. I remember long ago, in the late 1930s, telephoning my brother Blair when he was a student at Harvard. "I went to Hyannis last weekend to visit Jack Kennedy," he told me. I hadn't heard of Jack Kennedy. "Who is he?" I asked. "Oh, you know," he said, "the Ambassador's son." He told me about Jack's mother, Rose, giving him a lift back to Cambridge in her car, and asking him whether he thought the people of Boston would ever accept Catholics like the Kennedys socially. "What a ridiculous question!" Blair said, "I was 19, from New Jersey. How would I know?"

This was the first I heard of Jack Kennedy, but of course we all heard about him a great deal in the years afterward. When Kennedy was elected to President, he offered my bother Blair, who was by then a journalist of some distinction with CBS, the Ambassadorship to Morocco. In the same week, Blair was offered the job of Vice President of CBS News, and he opted for the latter position. Blair promoted Walter Cronkite to anchor of the CBS Evening News.

The early 1960s were exciting for all of us. We felt that anything was possible. Then came the day. I was alone on November 23, 1963, when Jackson phoned with the news. President John F. Kennedy had been shot in Dallas. Choking back tears, I watched Cronkite describing the scene in Texas and, finally, announcing that Kennedy was dead.

Life went on after the assassination. I was absorbed in my teaching. But slowly, something else, other concerns, began to seep in around the edges of my life.

Jackson and I often played tennis with Bob and Helen Meyner. Bob had been governor of New Jersey for two terms from 1953 to 1961. One Sunday in 1967, after our weekly game, Helen told me that she had given $100 to a group working against the Vietnam War. She urged me to do the same. The war wasn't front and center in people's consciousness at that point, but it was escalating, slowly but surely. I hated to watch the evening news, which always started out with a body count from the war. Jackson forbade me to give anything to the peace effort, declaring the very idea unpatriotic. But I remembered my professor at Smith who had taught us that a nationalistic patriotism had been one of the causes of World War I. I gave $100 to the peace group.

Up until Kennedy's presidency, I had been a registered Republican, even though I had supported Democrats on the national level. But the times were changing and as I became more and more informed of the struggles of the American people, I switched my party allegiance to the Democrats; a decision I proudly reaffirm every election day.

Around this time, some of my friends were working with the Civil Rights Movement led by Dr. Martin Luther King Jr., who spoke forcefully against the Vietnam War as well as racial injustice at home. In 1967, I was also asked to head a fundraising campaign for North Country School. The school had been wonderful for Roger, and I felt I owed a great deal to the Clarks.

I left my teaching job at Mary Mason's school to take on the fundraising job for North Country. It was a lucky move, one that would stand me in good stead for a political career, that unbeknownst to me, was opening up before me.

Chapter Seven

The 1960s had started out with such great promise when John F. Kennedy was elected President. His youth, vigor, and vision inspired the nation. Then, so quickly, it was overwhelmed by turbulence—the Cuban missile crisis, JFK's assassination, the Vietnam War, the race riots that tore apart America's cities. For those of us who were living then, it seemed as though the country was ready to explode, as if it would at any moment, fly apart.

I hated to watch the evening news or even to read the newspapers. It seemed to me that every day, on the front page of the *New York Times*, I was reading about two different wars. They were both taking place in Vietnam, but depending upon who was talking, they were taking entirely different courses. The stories from the paper's correspondents in that hapless country told of a war that was dragging on with little success and tremendous loss of life, more than 58,000 dead and 350,000 casualties in the end. But the stories quoting U.S. administration and military officials depicted a war we were winning. There was only once conclusion I could draw. It seemed, I told my brother Blair, that our government was lying to us.

And then there was the war at home. The news was full of stories and footage of the violence breaking out in America's urban ghettos. Who can forget those photographs of the smoke rising from our inner cities, the devastated blocks, the buildings torn and demolished, as though a tsunami had swept through?

When Roger was seven, he asked me, "Will I live to

grow up?" It had seemed a poignant question at the time, but it reverberated in my mind. Roger was one year away from college; he was draft age. He'd grown up, with his peers, living under the threat of nuclear annihilation. Now he, like his contemporaries, was faced with the decision of whether to go to college or to go and fight an unpopular war.

I lived like an ostrich. Many people did until the draft card came in the mail. There wasn't a clear path to political engagement for many of us at that point. I tried to deny what was happening and focused on North Country School and the fundraising campaign I was leading, which went so well that we ultimately raised twice the amount we had been aiming for.

Fundraising is initially a daunting task, but I was lucky to have been taken under the wing of a true master who was the professional fundraiser for the North Country school who taught me how to solicit funds from school parents. The hardest part, I would learn, is picking up the phone. I became a very good fundraiser because I enjoyed talking to people who shared my enthusiasm for the school. This would prove to be very useful later when I entered politics and had to raise money for candidates and for my own run for the New Jersey Senate.

One day in 1967, the phone rang. It was my bother Blair, just back from Europe, and calling with the news that would change my life. "I'm on my way to talk to Senator Eugene McCarthy," he said. McCarthy, a senator from Minnesota, first elected to office in 1958, was the author of several books and many poems. He opposed the war in Vietnam and was gearing up to run for the Democratic Presidential nomination against Lyndon Johnson as a means to stop the war. He wanted Blair to chair his campaign and Blair accepted.

I wanted to help Blair and do my part to end the war. I was so worried about our young men; many boys seemed to be dropping out of society, getting into drugs, turning away from life. Blair and I agreed that if something wasn't done about the war, we could lose a whole generation. Blair gave me the name of a friend of his, Nancy Wood, who also lived in Princeton and was raising money for the McCarthy campaign. With the experience I'd picked up from fundraising for North Country School, Blair thought I could be of valuable assistance to her.

I called her and she invited me over right away. Her dining room was littered with dozens of boxes filled with the names, addresses, and telephone numbers of New Jersey residents who might be willing to give time or money to McCarthy's campaign. I felt I'd embarked on an exciting crusade. I had rarely felt so needed or useful. What we were doing may have seemed quixotic to many on the outside, but we were convinced that if we worked hard enough and long enough, we could make a difference.

Nancy and I rode the crest of it, organizing money–raising events of all sorts, trying to be creative and squeeze as many dollars out of potential donors as we could. We came up with the idea of a loose–leaf notebook of drawings by New Jersey artists, which we had printed up and sold for $100 a copy. Our typical small fundraisers were $25–a head get–togethers for wine and cheese and some lively antiwar discussion. Sometimes we produced a "name" speaker; sometimes we spoke ourselves. Amazingly, although I was tentative and shy at first, I gradually found that I enjoyed speaking before a group and that I had some ability for it. And since I felt so passionately about the war, the task was easier.

On one occasion, Nancy asked if I could host a reception with George Kennan for a group of contributors, for which we would ask a $100 donation. I agreed, and it was an evening I'll never forget. George Kennan had been the originator of the policy of containment of the Soviet Union under President Truman. In 1946, Kennan was the Deputy Chief of Mission of the United States to the USSR under Ambassador W. Averell Harriman. Author of the famed *Long Telegram*, Kennan explained that the Soviet Union did not want to coexist with the West and that their focus was on the expansion of the Soviet system around the world; thus forming the bedrock of American Cold War policy.

By the time I first met him, George Kennan has changed much of his thinking about containment and was a professor at the Institute for Advanced Study in Princeton, having left the State Department in 1950. When George arrived at my house, he was taken aback to find nearly a hundred people in my living room. Jackson himself was nowhere to be found. While he enjoyed entertaining, he really only wanted to entertain those he considered to be VIPs or those who could be beneficial to Jackson Martindell, Inc. These "peaceniks" I had invited over were hardly important, so he sulked upstairs.

Kennan, standing before the fire, opened his remarks by saying that he had been diffident about coming because he had never had anything to do with political parties. But he was there now, he said, because he admired McCarthy's honesty and courage in putting himself on the front line to face a potentially devastating situation for our nation. The war, he said, was taxing our resources and draining our strength. The country was headed, he declared, toward the "greatest national humiliation" we had ever faced. You would think that we would learn from our mistakes, but as America forges ahead with its flawed and reprehensible war in Iraq, I fear the same prophecy ringing in my ears.

I was stunned by his speech and the picture—so prophetic, as it turned out—that he painted of our future. McCarthy was slowly making inroads, winning over doubters.

Some of my friends and acquaintances had been working
in the civil rights movement and believed that the antiwar
movement was a distraction, that it was a less important
cause than racial injustice in the United States. But some
of that changed in March 1967, when the Reverend Martin
Luther King Jr. led the first antiwar march after giving a
forceful speech against the war. His linkage of the two protest
movements was a critical milestone for the nation.

Early in 1968, Blair told me that he was trying to
persuade McCarthy to enter the New Hampshire primary.
The newspapers were full of accounts of the Tet offensive,
the Vietnamese response to General Westmoreland's strategy
to inflict heavy losses on the Vietcong. From the Vietnamese
point of view it was not only a military disaster, but a public
relations triumph. Walter Cronkite flew out to Vietnam
himself to report directly from the front. I watched his
program as he predicted that the best America could hope for
in the war was a stalemate, and that the only real solution
would be a negotiated settlement. This was the first time
Cronkite had voiced such an opinion about the war. Cronkite
was the most impressive and important news commentator
of my generation. It was becoming clear that a country with
limited resources had defeated our technologically superior
American force.

Up in New Hampshire, Blair and his staff were gearing
up. Sam Brown, a Harvard Divinity student, had gotten
in touch with McCarthy and offered to recruit hundreds of
young people from colleges and universities across the country
to volunteer. "The Kids," as they came to be called, turned
out to be extraordinary crusaders. They believed in McCarthy
and the platform, and they were willing to make sacrifices.
In New Hampshire, Blair and his staff were able only to give
them enough money for food. They slept wherever they could
find a place to lie down—on gymnasium floors, in church

basements, garages, and barns. Instructed to be "Clean for
Gene," they shaved their beards and wore clean, tidy clothes.
This was the first time that so many students had been
mobilized in a presidential campaign.

The Kids may have been paid paltry sums, but keeping
them going cost the campaign a great deal. Nancy and I, and
many other women like us, raised thousands upon thousands
of dollars to defray the costs and to hire the buses that took
the students to New Hampshire and elsewhere around the
country. Blair's staff organized them as precinct workers
statewide. They were given canvassing packets and sent off to
call on every registered voter, to each of whom they gave six
pieces of literature. This was my introduction on how to run a
political campaign and there was no better short course.

President Johnson's forces were unconcerned. They'd
never seen a campaign like this and didn't believe it would
work. Smugly, they predicted that McCarthy might get 10
percent of the vote.

On the evening of the New Hampshire primary, Nancy
and I were glued to the television set. As the vote tallies
trickled in, McCarthy's vote, unbelievably, kept growing.
Amazingly, by the time it was over, Johnson had won the
primary by only 230 votes. The Boston Globe's headline the
next morning read: "McCarthy's New Hampshire Dream
Becomes LBJ's Nightmare."

From then on, McCarthy began to get serious attention
and to develop real momentum. Many politicians tried to
coax Bobby Kennedy to back McCarthy, but he wouldn't do
it. Friends of Bobby now saw that Johnson was vulnerable
and urged Bobby to run even more vehemently. In March,
1967, Bobby Kennedy announced his candidacy for President.
Meanwhile, Blair and his staff flew out to Wisconsin to try
to convince McCarthy to divvy up the remaining primaries
with Kennedy, so as not to dissipate the antiwar forces. But

McCarthy would have none of it. Nancy and I were uneasy about all these political machinations. Gene McCarthy was our hero. To us, Bobby Kennedy was nothing but a spoiler at that time.

The evening of March 31, 1968, Nancy and I were sitting in front of the TV. Johnson was going to address the nation. It was an extraordinary moment when he spoke. He would not seek the nomination, he announced; he would not run for a second term. We were momentarily stunned. A sitting President had essentially given up his office.

Suddenly, Nancy leaped up and started jumping for joy. Now the only candidates left were Hubert Humphrey— who wouldn't come out against the war—Bobby Kennedy and McCarthy. She thought we had a real chance for the nomination.

But it was too soon to celebrate. Just a few days later, on April 3, Martin Luther King, Jr. was assassinated. All over the nation, violence erupted as black Americans expressed their justified rage. Kennedy seized the moment. He walked in the ruins in Washington. He campaigned vigorously by train in Indiana, ending his campaign speech with the famous paraphrase of George Bernard Shaw: "Some men see things as they are and say, Why? I dream of things that never were and say, Why not?" McCarthy did nothing. He just sulked.

Despite Kennedy's decision to throw his hat into the ring and despite his growing popularity, our anti–war volunteers were enthusiastic and encouraged. Nancy and I organized events all over New Jersey. We arranged for congressmen, senators, and other luminaries to tour the state and speak to our groups. Offers of help poured in from housewives, Princeton professors, and students.

We organized a $1,000–a–plate dinner for McCarthy at the Ramada Inn in New Brunswick. The "Great Man" was coming to dinner, accompanied on his swing through New

Jersey by Congressman Frank "Thompy" Thompson, an effective liberal and a leader in the congressional Democratic Study Group who had tried, as had George McGovern, to persuade Bobby Kennedy to support McCarthy.

The dinner was held in the Don Quixote Room. My friend, former Governor Bob Meyner, teased me about the name of our venue. "It's appropriate," he said, "since you're tilting at windmills."

A small but enthusiastic crowd greeted McCarthy in the parking lot. But McCarthy seemed dreary. He was beautiful to look at, just as he had seemed on TV at the 1960 convention when he gave one of the nominating speeches for Adlai Stevenson. Then he had seemed magical. But as the evening unfolded, I searched in vain for that same magic. Where had it gone? When McCarthy spoke, he still said all the things I believed about the war, but he said them in a flat voice, completely lacking in passion and fire. He seemed to be sleepwalking. We didn't know it at the time, but McCarthy was suffering from depression; he himself called his ailment "acedia" (or spiritual sloth).

Nine primaries had followed New Hampshire. Bobby and Gene had gone head to head in Indiana, and Bobby won. He won again in Nebraska. On May 28, the crucial primary in Oregon was to take place. Blair called me and stressed the importance of that contest. He said he was giving the campaign a major contribution and asked what I could do to help.

I hardly stopped to think. "I could manage $50,000," I said.

Blair spent $100,000 buying radio time in Oregon, and Gene became more assertive about the differences between himself and Bobby Kennedy. When the returns came in, Blair called me, ecstatic. McCarthy had won the Oregon primary, with 44.7 percent of the vote to 38.8 percent for Kennedy. It

was the first time in twenty–two years that a Kennedy had
lost any kind of election, and Kennedy announced that if he
was beaten in California the following week, he would drop
out of the race.

This, of course, is not what happened. Kennedy won
the California primary, and it seemed the nomination race was
over. I was crushed, listening to his victory speech. Kennedy
asked McCarthy's troops to join him in bringing change to
the nation. I shouted at the television set. It was quarter past
three in morning, Princeton time.

As Bobby exited the hotel ballroom, I suddenly heard
a reporter shout, "Senator Kennedy has been shot!" My
heart seemed to stop. I sat frozen in front of the set, feeling
terribly alone. Jackson was away and it was too late to call
Nancy or Blair. I hoped, in any case, they weren't watching.
Feeling suddenly terribly hopeless, I burst into tears. "What's
happening to our country?" I cried.

*   *   *   *   *

In August of 1968, Nancy Wood and I were
sitting in our room in a hotel overlooking Lincoln Park in
Chicago. We had come to Chicago, with our sons, for the
Democratic Convention, the culmination of all we had been
working so hard for over the last year. George, my eldest, had
also come all the way from Seattle, at his own expense. We
knew McCarthy would not get the Democratic nomination,
but we wanted to be there to witness this historic occasion
for ourselves. Nancy and I brought the younger boys along
thinking it would be a wonderful education for them to see the
democratic process at work.

Suddenly, Allen, Nancy's 19–year–old son, burst in.
"Roger!" he shouted. "Come look out the window—the police

are beating up students in the park!" Roger, now 17, preceded me into the room next door. From the window, we watched the police, nightsticks flailing, attack the young people camping out in the park. I could hardly believe my eyes. When I was young, I remembered Nanny telling me that a policeman was always your friend. Were these blue–coated men the ones she had been talking about? I wondered what kind of education it would be.

Nancy told us that Chicago Mayor Richard Daley had told his police that the young people gathering in their city were dangerous Communists intent on overthrowing the government. Most of the students, as I understood it, only wanted to request permission to march to the convention hall with thousands of sheets of paper, representing tens of thousands of signatures, from people opposed to the war. They hoped to present their signatures to the delegates to urge them to vote for the peace plank in the party platform.

That afternoon, I called Helen Meyner, Bob Meyner's wife, at the Palmer House Hotel. She and Bob were members of the New Jersey delegation, headed by Governor Richard J. Hughes, who chaired the credentials committee. Helen was writing a column for the *Newark Star Ledger*, New Jersey's largest daily.

"Helen," I said. "I've been out on the street and in the park. The police are just awful; they're beating up all the young people. No wonder our kids say you can't trust anyone over thirty."

Helen didn't believe me. She thought I was exaggerating. The police were being very polite, she said; the problem was the media, who were stirring up trouble. I invited her to come out with me to see for herself what was going on.

Leaving the Palmer House, we walked about three blocks before a policeman swinging a nightstick accosted us, demanding to know what we were doing.

"Just walking, officer," Helen said. The policeman ordered us off the street, and then pushed us into the entrance of a building and up against a wall. Helen protested that she was Governor Meyner's wife, but the policeman only retorted, "Governor, nothing," and proceeded to frisk us. He made us open our pocketbooks—presumably to check for weapons.

Helen, appalled, described the policeman's behavior in her column the next day, upsetting her husband, who feared that readers would think his wife was a radical liberal, hurting his chances in the gubernatorial race he had just entered.

At dusk Nancy and I went to Grant Park to find a good vantage point to watch a peace march that consisted of a group of delegates pledged to McCarthy. All over the city, streets were lined with tanks and jeeps, with rows of barbed wire strung across the hoods. Roger wondered aloud if this was a war, and if so, who was the enemy?

As we walked into the park, we saw two policemen, not much older than our boys, standing back-to-back under a street lamp. Protesters were shouting at them, hurling invectives: "Pigs! Fascists!" As the policemen lashed out at the young protestors with their nightsticks, they looked like frightened children themselves.

It was getting dark. I was scared. I told Nancy we should go back to the hotel, and the atmosphere seemed ominous, as though anything might happen. But Nancy insisted we stay.

Off in the distance, we could hear singing, "The Battle Hymn of the Republic." The sound got louder, and the marchers swung into sight, each one carrying a candle flickering bravely in the gloom. Our New Jersey delegation came into view led by my young friend Dan Gaby. Woody Guthrie's "This land is Your land," was sung followed by "We Shall Overcome," the theme song of the Civil Rights Movement in which many of them had participated. Suddenly it struck me how strange it was that the President they hated, Lyndon Johnson, was the very man who had done so much for civil rights. But I joined in the singing, along with Nancy, and tears ran down our cheeks.

*   *   *   *   *

Nancy and I managed to get tickets to the convention the following day, but we weren't able to get any for our sons. We went over to McCarthy headquarters, where they were working, and made them promise to stay there and not go out into the streets or march with the protestors. They agreed. Bitterly, Roger told us that whenever they went out, the police told them to move along and pushed and jostled them, "just because we're young." It didn't make any difference that their hair was short and they wore shirts and ties. Youth seemed to be the enemy.

The convention hall was surrounded by what looked to be miles of barbed wire. For us McCarthy supporters, the peace plank proposed for the platform had been the most important issue before the convention, but it had already gone down to defeat. Hubert Humphrey, Johnson's Vice President and the presumptive nominee, would not endorse it. Loyalty to his President had made him a captive of a failed policy.

Still, Nancy and I wanted to be present for the proceedings of the day. We were early and took our seats in the balcony. "Isn't it a strange atmosphere?" Nancy remarked. "I'm a little scared." After the defeat of the peace plank, it seemed that Daley's minions had increased their violence. Prominent newsmen like Dan Rather and Mike Wallace were pushed around on the convention floor by security forces.

The convention opened with the Star Spangled Banner

and the Pledge of Allegiance. But just a few minutes into the proceedings, a McCarthy delegate suddenly rushed up and grabbed a microphone. "Children are being beaten in the streets," he shouted. I'll never forget how my heart rose into my throat. Nancy and I had the same, single thought. Where were our sons?

We rushed down the steps of the balcony. John Kenneth Galbraith was running toward us. He grabbed my hand. I told him I needed to know if Roger was safe. Nancy and I commandeered a taxi to take us to McCarthy headquarters at the Blackstone Hotel. As we raced along, the radio blared reports of police chasing demonstrators, throwing them into paddy wagons, bruised and bloody.

By the time we got to headquarters, Nancy and I were in tears. Blair wasn't there. Neither was Roger or Allen Wood. My nephew Tim, Blair's son, was sitting white-faced on a chair, his shirt torn and a cut on his forehead. "Where's Blair? What happened?" I nearly screamed.

"The police came in here, threw us against the wall and frisked us," Tim said, his voice shaking. "They called us dirty Communists." Blair, he said, had gone out to check the local hospitals for the kids.

Nearly six long hours later, around 10 o'clock that night, Roger and Allen finally got through the police cordon surrounding the hotel and came up to the 10th floor to find us. Roger's blue eyes were black, his pupils enormous from the fumes of the mace sprayed by the police.

Roger told us what had happened. He and Allen, bored at headquarters, had gone out to see what the demonstrators were doing. From what they could see, the protestors were quietly waiting while their leaders asked for permission to formally present their anti-war petitions to the convention. The boys stood on the sidewalk, watching them. A battalion of police, supplemented with National Guard, stood across the street, with tanks on either side of them.

"Suddenly, without any warning, none at all, they charged into the sitting students and in our direction," Allen said. And then both boys were talking at once, their words tumbling out. "They sprayed mace, they beat them with nightsticks, and they kicked them. They grabbed them and threw them into paddy wagons. We ran. Fast." Both athletes, the boys had escaped, but the mace had gotten into their eyes.

I was relieved that nothing had happened to my son, but the events of the convention had indelibly changed me. The *Trenton Times* reported that I had been "radicalized." And I supposed they were right, at least for a time. I felt the need to work, and work hard, to change public opinion, to prevent more young men from being sent off to a war that was tearing the nation apart.

Eugene McCarthy was more a poet than a politician. He approached political problems from that perspective. He was at the outset a brave man, risking his own political future by challenging a sitting President of his own party. Some thought he did not take the campaign seriously, but there is no question that he was serious about stopping the war in Vietnam. And there is no question that he had a passionate and dedicated campaign organization.

On the other hand, Bobby Kennedy was a natural politician, experienced and savvy. McCarthy was cool; Kennedy was hot. As money was always a problem, the McCarthy campaign was a Rolls Royce effort on a jalopy budget. Kennedy had access to plenty of money and experienced political experts. McCarthy had thousands of youngsters, starry–eyed and "Clean for Gene." In this pre–Internet era, McCarthy had tapped the energy and commitment of America's youth.

The two major political issues at the 1968 Convention were the Vietnam War and the nomination of a presidential candidate. The McCarthy and Kennedy supporters had lost their candidates; Kennedy to assassination and McCarthy to depression. The political operatives maneuvered among the delegates attempting to persuade Hubert Humphrey to support the so–called "peace plank" platform. President Johnson wanted Humphrey to be the nominee, but he also wanted Humphrey to support his position to continue the Vietnam War. The regular Democrats supported Humphrey, so Johnson's policy triumphed with Humphrey's nomination. With McCarthy unable to lead and Kennedy deceased, the anti–war forces were left fractured and leaderless.

On the final day of the convention, a film tribute to Bobby Kennedy was shown. Norman Mailer described it succinctly: "Even dead, and on film, he was better and more moving than anything. People were crying, an ovation began. Delegates came to their feet and applauded an empty screen. It was as if the center of American life was now passing the age when it could still look forward; now people looked back into memory, into the past of the nation."

The events of 1968 hit hard. Many politicians, frightened by the television images of the Chicago convention, actually became cautious and more conservative. As a result, the influence of the right grew stronger in both parties. It marked a turning point in our country.

I did not know it at the time but I was going to have a part in fighting against the political turn toward conservatism. What I did know was that I had found something that I loved doing, something that I felt I had been born to do. It was more than half my life in coming, but it had come at last at 56 years old.

These events would shape the path of my political engagement as I could no longer ignore the need to get involved to help fight for what I knew was right.

Anne, and her brothers, Blair and Bill, 1928, New York City.

Anne, September, 1933.

Anne and Jackson Martindell 1953, Princeton.

Anne with her son George Scott, 1965, London.

As Director of the Office of International Disaster Relief, Anne Martindell
traveled around the world to regions in distress. Here she is in Southern India.
The writing on the blackboard, below, analyzes the availability of supplies.

Vice President Walter Mondale swears in Anne Martindell as new U.S. Ambassador to New Zealand and Western Samoa, July 25, 1979 in Washington, D.C., as her granddaughter, Katherine Luther, holds a Bible. (AP Photo)

Ambassador Martindell aboard a small craft to visit the island of Atafu in the South Pacific, 1980.

Arriving in Antarctica in Ambassador Martindell is nicknamed 'Antarctic Annie.' As Ambassador to New Zealand, Martindell traveled extensively to improve and maintain positive relations between the U. S. and New Zealand.

Toss Woollaston, seen here standing before Wellington harbor, is regarded as one of New Zealand's foremost landscape painters. He was Anne Martindell's true love.

Ambassador Martindell meeting Prince Charles in New Zealand. He held her hand for eight minutes. (Dominion newspaper photo)

Sailing with Walter Cronkite in 1990. Anne's brother Blair, promoted Cronkite to anchor at CBS.

Anne Martindell with Bill and Hillary Clinton on the campaign trail, 1996.

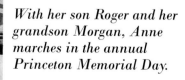

With her son Roger and her grandson Morgan, Anne marches in the annual Princeton Memorial Day.

Receiving assistance from Smith advisor, Dan Horowitz, with her graduation cap.

With Congressman Rush Holt at Anne's 90th birthday.

With President Jimmy Carter at a meeting of The Carter Center, Cambridge, MA, 2007.

Chapter Eight

My own political life started soon after the Democratic Convention in 1968 when Bob Meyner, who ran the following year for a third term as governor of New Jersey, tapped me to be vice–chairman of the Democratic Party in New Jersey. With a formidable opponent in Republican William Cahill, he had worried that all my "liberal and peacenik friends," as he put it, would sit on their hands during the campaign and cost him the election. Putting me in a position of responsibility in the party would be a way, as he saw it, of ensuring that the more liberal wing of the party would be brought along to work for him.

For the next few days I was dizzy with excitement. I could scarcely believe this was happening to me. But then, that's how my life had been for the last four years, one I could never have imagined for myself twenty years earlier. Once again, just as when I had been asked to teach, I found myself invited to do something I really knew nothing about. I didn't know the first thing about party politics. But I've always been eager to learn and I'm a quick study. So I'd taken on the job and thrown myself into it.

What I learned right away was that there was a stark divide between the male and the female roles in the party. The men in those days didn't expect or want women to think; they just wanted them to pour the coffee and stuff the envelopes and be happy with little pats on the head for the good work, while they, the men, made all the significant and substantive decisions. In my role as vice–chairman, I found the party men courteous toward me, even deferential, but as I told one reporter: "They open doors for me and carry my briefcase, but they won't listen to any serious ideas from a woman."

I was horrified at the idea that there was a "woman's division" in the party. I considered it a female ghetto. I was very naïve; I thought I had a real job and that I would be part of the decision–making process. I quietly hoped to change the situation in the party. Wherever I went, speaking chiefly to women's groups, attending luncheons and fundraisers, I would try to stir up the ladies who were stuffing envelopes, manning tables, and preparing food. The men got what they wanted— power—but what did the women get, beyond perhaps a focus for their social lives? I would talk to the women about the division of power, and my goal of increasing women's duties and utilizing more of their talents, getting them involved in discussions on issues, the party programs and legislative problems.

Bob Meyner lost the gubernatorial election that year, but the vice–chairman had a four–year term, so I had ample opportunity to keep pressing on with my plans. In my second year, I learned that my boss, the state chairman, a man named Sal Bontempo, had called a meeting of the "Big Bulls" of the state Democratic Party to discuss the reform rules of a national commission. Chaired by Senator George McGovern, this commission was attempting to repair the damage the party had suffered in the previous years.

I called Sal and told him I wanted to be at the meeting. "The boys don't want any women there," Sal replied. But I wasn't going to be dissuaded. I suppose it was anger that gave me courage as I got in my car and drove north. As I arrived outside Sal's gated home, I ran into U.S. Senator Pete Williams, who walked with me to the door. This was lucky, and gave me courage; I knew the men wouldn't throw him out. As soon as my presence was announced, we could hear Sal roar: "She doesn't know the meaning of party discipline!"

Pete looked at me with a puzzled expression but opened the door and politely stood aside for me to enter. Knees knocking, I stepped into the room. There they were, all the big bulls of the Democratic Party of New Jersey, men accustomed to controlling the political destiny of most of the citizens of the state. They were standing in a circle in Sal's living room, smoking and drinking. No one, certainly no woman, had ever questioned their authority.

Looking past Sal's glare, I saw Bob Meyner and Dick Hughes, both of them former governors, and the democratic chairmen of the state's six largest counties. Bob's hawk face had embarrassment written all over it. Dick's cherubic features were creased into a smile he was trying to hide. I took a deep breath.

"I've studied these rules," I told Sal, my voice shaking. "And I've come to represent the nearly 600 Democratic committee women. We have a right to know what you're discussing."

For several moments there was dead silence. Sal glowered at me. Then Tony Grossi, the oldest and most charming of the county chairmen, spoke up.

"Anne, we boys all like you," he said. "But when we get together, we sometimes use rough language. We wouldn't want to offend you."

I looked him right in the eye. "I don't give a shit what kind of language you use," I said, hardly believing my own ears. I'd never used that word publicly before.

There was a stunned silence for a few seconds. I could see Dick Coffee, my county chairman, choking back his laughter. Then everyone broke out into guffaws.
"Sit down, Anne, for God's sake, and have a drink,"
Bob Meyner said. I took a seat. For the rest of the meeting the men ignored me, but I was never excluded again as far as I know.

The next day, accounts of my comments at the meeting were on the front pages of nearly every newspaper in the state. Dick Coffee had apparently told the story to his favorite reporters, who loved it, although not all of them got the story quite straight. Some reported the offending word as much stronger than the one I had used, while others speculated on precisely which word had issued from my mouth. Later that night, my mother called to say she was proud of what I did, but also not proud of what I had said. The story gave me quick prominence. Suddenly, I wasn't just an obscure party vice–chairman toiling in the boondocks. I was a bona fide political figure in New Jersey. Maybe that's how you rise to the top in New Jersey politics!

By the time Dick Coffee asked me to run for the State Senate, I had run George McGovern's successful presidential campaign in New Jersey and been labeled by *Washington Post* columnist Joseph Alsop the *"Boadicea of New Jersey"*—the Celtic queen with her body painted blue, because I was the woman who had helped the loonies of the left shanghai the Democratic Party.

Of course, nobody expected me actually to win the senate race. The Republican incumbent, Bill Schluter, was very popular, essentially a shoo–in to be reelected. And the largest part of the district, Hunterdon County, was staunchly Republican. But the Democrats needed a candidate, and so far no one had been willing to take on a losing effort. Maybe they thought I wouldn't know any better, and that's why I was asked; but I have to admit that it didn't take very long to convince me. We madly gathered signatures for the next two days and I filed with two hours to spare.

At the Democratic Convention in Miami in 1972, I stood on the podium with George McGovern as he accepted the Democratic nomination for President. And my own name had even been put into the hat for Vice President, as the women's caucus promoted me and Sissy Farenthold of Texas as one of the possible candidates for McGovern to select as his running mate. McGovern, of course, infamously selected first Missouri Senator Thomas Eagleton, who was forced to withdraw when it came out that he had once been treated for depression in the past. Kennedy brother–in–law Sargent Shriver replaced Eagleton.

Despite all this, my name recognition among ordinary voters in New Jersey was undeniably low. I had to work hard to raise people's awareness but I did so diligently. In no time, I learned that I loved campaigning. I loved meeting people and talking with them about their concerns; I even loved appearing before groups, large or small, and making campaign speeches. It was amazing to think that I, shy Anne Clark, who had moved through life so painfully for so many years, had matured to this point of confidence and liberation.

I visited supermarkets, nursing homes, and knocked on doors. Everywhere I heard the same complaints—property taxes were too high, inflation was eating away at people's salaries and their purchasing power, traffic problems were endemic, new roads were needed. I debated my Republican opponent on taxes in a David and Goliath encounter—and I did surprisingly well. My secretary at the time was also a terrific policy analyst, especially regarding taxation, and could brief me on what would otherwise be a rather esoteric subject.

By this time, the Watergate investigation was in full swing, but it wasn't something I heard about very much from my potential constituents. I was acutely aware of it myself, however. On the Fourth of July, when I listened to the Declaration of Independence being read aloud before a traditional parade in Hunterdon County, I thought how perilously close we as a people had come to losing our right to liberty and the pursuit of happiness during these years with

Richard Nixon as our President. It was nothing compared to what would happen during the George W. Bush presidency.

Then, three weeks before our New Jersey elections, Nixon fired Archibald Cox, the special prosecutor who had been appointed to look into the Watergate scandal. I'd been prepared to be a sacrificial lamb for my party, but now it seemed as if I had a real chance of being elected.

My district was heavily Republican, but campaigning the day after Cox's firing I was greeted by a woman who shook my hand enthusiastically and declared that, even though she was a lifelong Republican, she was now ashamed of her party and the President. "I'm going to vote for you," she said. The same thing happened over and over. When I drove along in my Ford LTV, festooned with the red, white and blue "Anne Martindell for State Senate" sign, strangers now waved and tooted their horns.

On election night, I had invited people to come to what I had thought would be a wake at my Battle Road house in Princeton, expecting the worst. But I squeezed past Schluter with almost 2 percent more votes. My brother Blair, who'd managed my campaign, was ecstatic. My mother was thrilled. I was incredulous but never more excited or happy in my life.

The Legislature met in Trenton Mondays and Thursdays. Committees met in the morning. Then the full sessions met at two in the afternoon, continuing until all bills posted on the board were voted upon or postponed. Generally, the sessions lasted until five or six o'clock in the evening.

My desk in the chamber was in the center of the third row. Senator Steve Wylie sat on my left and next to him sat Senator Winona Lipman, a dignified compassionate black woman serving her second term. We were three of the five liberals in the body, and Winona, Alene Ammond, and I were the three women in the New Jersey Senate. We females had more forces on the other side of the State House—six women served in the lower house, the assembly.

On one of the first days of my term, Winona smiled at me. "Let's go up to the balcony," she said. "I'll show you the new ladies' room I got them to install."

"What did you use before that?" I asked her.

"I had to go out through the lines of lobbyists and down the hall to the public toilets," she said laughing and described how the lobbyists would all accost her as she tried to make a beeline for the restroom. I asked her how she'd ever managed to get the state to install a ladies' room for so few female legislators. She grinned at me. "Persistence," she said.

It's amazing to think that in those days, a quarter of a century ago, there were a total of only 37 female state senators in all the state houses around the country. Today, of course, there are literally thousands. According to the Center for American in Politics, in 2007, 1,734, or 23.5 percent, of the 7,382 state legislators in the United States were women. Women hold 423, or 21.5 percent, of the 1,971 state senate seats and 1,311, or 24.2 percent, of the 5,411 state house seats. We've come a long way, but not far enough.

I served in the New Jersey State Senate for a single four–year term. It was an exhilarating period of my life, full of purpose and meaning. For the first time in my public life I felt I was making a concrete, measurable difference, even though the experience could be extremely frustrating. The compromises and deal making in politics are never pretty; there is a saying: "Like sausage, you don't want to watch laws being made." In the beginning, I struggled to make my voice heard. My fellow senators, with a few exceptions, felt that women should stay at home, minding their manners and their families. It was a balancing act to promote programs and ideas without being so aggressive that the men would react negatively. I found that I could draw on my experience of inn keeping at Mont Gabriel to deal with my colleagues with diplomacy. And my upbringing had inculcated a certain amount of good manners, which paid off as well.

Politics, and for that matter legislating, is part compromise, part bargaining, part persuasion. I found I had a knack for the give and take required to forward my agenda items. It came easily to me, the nurturing and cajoling. What gave me pause, though, was just how alluring politics could be, how tempting it could be to use the political arena to forward an agenda for personal benefit rather than in service to the public good. I persevered the best I could, trying not to let it all change me. I had my share of failures, but I had some triumphs, too.

My committee assignments were education and appropriations, but most of my time was spent on education. In the first two–year session I was chair of the Subcommittee on Higher Education, in the second I chaired the entire committee when the chairman, Senator Wylie took a six–month leave of absence while he was being considered for an appointment to the State Supreme Court.

My first legislative act was to prepare a resolution calling for the impeachment of President Richard Nixon. Nothing gave me more satisfaction. The Congressional Watergate Committee, chaired by New Jersey's Representative Peter Rodino, had already spent several months studying the tapes recorded in the White House. I called Rodino and told him of the resolution I planned. He was supportive, saying that if an impeachment resolution passed in our state legislature, it might help speed up action in Congress.

When I presented my resolution in caucus, Senator Tom Dunn spoke up right away to object. Dunn had been chairman of Democrats for Nixon. He had been wined and dined at the White House and now he felt he couldn't take any action hostile to the President. As he spoke, I sat there thinking, 'Aren't you ashamed that you, a lifelong Democrat, support this man?' Of course, I didn't say it out loud. I was still a good girl.

Senate President Pat Dodd, gave me a small lecture on senatorial courtesy. "It's the tradition of this body not to criticize any colleague or to place anyone in an embarrassing position," he said. "I don't think you'll want to put that resolution on the board."

New to the legislature and unused to its strange protocol, I allowed myself to be dissuaded from presenting my resolution. I've always regretted it. Richard Nixon resigned on August 8, 1974.

A year later, I remembered this experience when the newspapers devoted headlines and large columns of space to the rescue operation of the *Mayaguez*, a U.S. merchant ship that was captured in the Sea of Thailand by pirates. One of the senators drafted a resolution to send to President Gerald Ford, praising him for his courage in sending marines to rescue the ship. When one senator urged that the motion to carry this resolution be unanimous, I stood up.

"Forty–five marines were killed in that operation, and nearly eighty were wounded trying to rescue the thirty–nine crew members," I said. "In view of our heavy casualties, I believe this resolution is inappropriate."

Several other senators followed my lead. When the vote came, the resolution passed, but by no means unanimously. It wasn't the first time I had stood up to my colleagues. But it was the first time my opposition had an influence on my colleagues.

The *Mayaguez* incident played well for the administration in official Washington, too, although there were a few dissenting voices that recognized what ultimately came out in a General Accounting Office report—that President Ford had overreacted and shot from the hip, ignoring diplomatic messages saying that there was a good prospect for a peaceful resolution. Among the dissenters were George McGovern, Gaylord Nelson, and a new congresswoman from Colorado, Patricia Schroeder. Many years later, I met Pat when she was running for President. "I remembered what you had said about the Mayaguez when Reagan ordered the invasion of Grenada," she told me. "And then when Bush behaved the same way in Panama. They're all cowboys, aren't they? Do you think they'll ever grow up?"

I worked hard when I was on the Committee for Higher Education, dealing closely with the state chancellor, Ralph Dungan, who had restructured the teachers' colleges into four–year liberal arts institutions. I also worked closely with Ed Bloustein, President of Rutgers University, who had done an excellent job improving Rutgers, the oldest land grant college in the United States, turning it into one of the top state universities in the country. I held hearings when budget cuts were proposed, but it was difficult to find the money for improvements and even, in the end, for the status quo.

Public school issues were troubling. Our courts had mandated that all New Jersey children should have a "thorough and efficient" education, as guaranteed by the state constitution. But there was a wide disparity in funds spent per pupil between the affluent suburbs and the inner cities. I traveled around the state, visiting schools and meeting with school board members. I remember being shocked by my visit to Middlesex County, where the classrooms were kept locked and security guards patrolled the halls checking for drugs and weapons. Twenty–five years later, we still haven't solved the problems of either safety or equity in our school system.

One of the issues that got me attention was the fight over abortion. This became a very difficult, even painful issue for me since my personal feelings conflicted with the principle I felt had to be respected. My doctor, an old friend, told me

that he advised his unmarried pregnant patients to have
their babies, then put them up for adoption. Nevertheless,
I felt that every woman should have the right to make the
decision whether or not to bear a child. She should have the
right to make her decision in the privacy of her own heart
and conscience, after considering her own circumstances and
consulting with her doctor.

When one of my fellow senators introduced a resolution
calling on Congress to ban all abortions, the right–to–life
soldiers came out in force to the state house. You should have
seen them. They looked like women who gave tea parties, not
militant protesters. They were dressed to kill and packed the
balconies on the state house. Mustering all my courage, I led
the fight against the resolution. "A woman should have the
basic freedom of choice to determine whether or not to bear
children," I practically shouted, as boos and hisses rained
down on me from the spectator's balcony. "This state, this
nation, should neither advocate nor condemn abortion."

I tried not to listen to the clamor in the gallery. "If we
are going to dictate in every area," I continued, "let's legislate
stringent requirements for marriage and pay for parenthood
training. Let's have an effect on the growing numbers of
battered and abused children. Let's make a concerted effort
to disseminate birth control and adoption information and
increase day care."

Despite my efforts, only six of us voted against the
resolution. I was the only woman among the six: the other
two women in the Senate abstained, concerned that a "no"
vote would have killed them in their districts. I knew a "no"
vote would go over all right in Princeton, but the rest of my
district was very conservative. I was convinced I was only able
to have one term in any case, so I was determined to vote my
convictions.

And I did, repeatedly—against an obscenity bill I saw

as an attack on freedom of speech, and most importantly, against a death penalty bill I vigorously opposed and which we defeated in the 1975–76 legislative session. (It passed a few years later when I was out of the country.) I was horrified by living conditions in many of the nursing homes I had visited in the state and was determined to do something about them. So I sponsored a bill to allow municipalities to zone for senior citizen housing. It passed 35–0.

In 1974, during the energy crisis that created long lines at gas pumps around the nation, I proposed the creation of a Bureau of Energy Information in the State Energy Office, which would have subpoena powers to require oil companies to make detailed reports to the state. We still need this today. I was concerned that the oil companies, always in search of the almighty dollar, seemed to be diverting gasoline from New Jersey, one of the states hardest hit by the fuel shortage, to other states. My actions got me on the newspaper pages repeatedly. One newspaper wrote: "Senator Martindell is not running out of energy in her vigorous pursuit to ease the energy crisis and gas shortage," and praised my "high octane enthusiasm that New Jersey citizens would survive the energy crisis."

Another major battle in which I played a large role was over casino gambling. I was greatly opposed to this idea. As I saw it, legalizing gambling would poison the quality of life in the Garden State and detract from efforts to develop serious social and economic programs. It was nothing but a transparent attempt to sidestep much needed tax reform. The debate in the Senate over a bill calling for a public referendum on the issue, allowing casinos anywhere in New Jersey, was heated and the vote very close.

The campaign against casino gambling—we called it "Casinos No Dice"—was born in my living room three weeks later. We organized a grassroots movement to defeat the special interests and influence peddlers who had bought the legislature. I wanted to inject some fun and flamboyance into the campaign, so I took to wearing a wide–brimmed straw hat ringed with rubber dice, topped by a sign that said "NO" in large letters, whenever I made an appearance on the issue or was interviewed by the press or on television. "I've got my chips and cards out on the table," I'd say. The media loved it. So did I. I looked silly, I knew, but it didn't matter. I wanted to make my point, and I was making it in front of photographers all over the state.

We had our work cut out for us: though early polls had shown little support for gambling, the Atlantic City group trying to place casinos in that struggling city had been putting forth a great effort and a lot of money. By July, statewide polls showed 70 percent of voters were in favor of a casino referendum. My position obviously wasn't very popular, but I accepted my unpopularity as a badge of honor. The co–chairman of "Casinos No Dice," Ray Bateman, told me he thought I loved being the Christian in the arena with the lions. Maybe I did.

We worked long, and we worked hard. One afternoon a group of us went to Atlantic City and stood on the boardwalk in front of one of the old run–down hotels, the Chalfonte. It once was an elegant beach resort. My grandmother Clark had stayed there every spring to take in the sea air. The wind whipped about us as we faced the television cameras, the seedy buildings rising behind us. To our left were tumbledown, unpainted houses occupied by poor tenants we knew would be evicted if the referendum passed. Where, we asked, would they go? The notion that casinos would help the poor, we said, was blatantly false.

We made speeches all over the state. We held coffee parties. We talked to everyone and anyone who would stand still long enough to listen. We won some good endorsements

from prominent state politicians, including Republican
Senator Clifford Case and U.S. Attorney Jonathan Goldstein.

We knew the odds were against us. Late one evening in
October of 1974, I waited in my living room with my lawyer
for some callers who had requested a meeting. The doorbell
rang. I opened the door to two flashily–dressed men who had
just emerged from a long black limousine parked by the curb.
Out stepped the President of Resorts International, the
company hoping to open casinos in Atlantic City, and his
lawyer.

The meeting got off to an acrimonious start. The
Resorts lawyer informed me that the organization considered
statements I had made about it libelous and that they
intended to take "appropriate action" against me. Resorts
International, which operated casinos in the Bahamas, was
a legitimate business listed on the New York stock exchange.
But rumors about its allies and supporters—and its possible
Mafia connections—should have scared New Jersey citizens
out of their wits

"Let's talk about what you plan to do," I said. "You're
going to entice unwary and unsophisticated citizens to gamble
away their rent money, grocery money, or money they should
be spending on their children's shoes. You're trying to put the
state in the swindle business."

The Resorts executive glared at me as my lawyer
informed him that libel laws applied differently to campaign
statements and that they could never hope to win a suit
against me. "Very well, senator," he said as they got up to
leave. "But don't think there won't be consequences." I
thought I smelled a faint scent of sulfur.

A week or so later, I was driving south in the slow lane
of the Jersey Turnpike in my blue Mercedes with its "AMRI"
license plates, which indicated I was the senator from Mercer
County. A large black limousine with darkened windows

suddenly cut in front of me, forcing me out of my lane and into the path of an incoming truck. I barely managed to swerve out of the way to avoid what could have been a fatal collision. I don't know to this day whether the two events were related, but after that I didn't drive to New York on the turnpike until the campaign was over.

On election night, we watched the returns come in. We were prepared for a defeat, but as the votes were tallied we could hardly believe what we were seeing. We had defeated the referendum by nearly two to one. The dice had rolled our way, seven over eleven. "Casinos No Dice" had accomplished what had seemed to be the impossible. Or, as one letter writer put it to me in the missives of congratulations that poured in afterwards: "You tackled the job that couldn't be done, and you did it!"

I was proud of the victory, but it was short–lived. The next year, Resorts International reorganized its efforts and raised over a million dollars to fund its campaign. The legislature voted to put the casino question to a referendum once again and this time to restrict the casinos to Atlantic City only. Chairing the Education Committee, I didn't have the time to put into the anti–gambling effort again, and the voters, perhaps lulled by the thought that gambling in only one location could do little harm, gave the measure their approval. It was a sad day, I still believe, for New Jersey. But at least gambling was localized, rather than having slot machines in every grocery store and gas station.

Jackson could see how happy I was when I was completely engaged and loving what I was doing. He had seen that when I first began teaching. But when it became clear what kind of politics, and what kind of people I believed in—liberal, left, idealistic—he quickly lost interest. He thought my causes and my candidates hopeless and naïve, not to mention useless to him in his own ambitions.

I'm not sure if it's all true, or what the whole story is, but I suspect that Jackson had some affiliation with the CIA that may have forced him to distance himself from my political activities. Within the first month of our marriage, I was summoned to dinner with Jackson and Alan Dulles, then director of the CIA. Why Alan Dulles wanted to meet me remains a mystery to this day. I knew that during the Second World War Jackson had done some work in the intelligence field. I did find it odd that he told me he would only live in a house with two exits, so he could escape if necessary. And he was always reading spy novels. But I wonder if my liberal cronies were an embarrassment to Jackson and his sense of duty.

There were other important issues, exciting campaigns —creating a state income tax, fighting against the death penalty, and so much more. Life was busy, full, and good. But there was still a void in my life, one vital element missing —love.

My married life with Jackson was over. At the start of my political activities, Jackson had been enthusiastic, both because he thought it was important for me to have something concrete to do with my time and because he thought my involvement in politics might be of some benefit to him. Eventually, he abandoned me to my activities, while he pursued his own. It wasn't long before we were leading completely separate lives.

One day, Jackson called me from Fort Lauderdale. "Honey," he said, "I've just bought the most beautiful house, with a view of the inland waterway." Jackson always described any house, or for that matter, any woman he liked as the most beautiful in the world. "I want you to come see it right away. You'll want to move immediately," he insisted.

I protested. I couldn't move, I said, not just because of the job but because I could never be that far away from my children and friends.

Jackson kept pressing until ultimately, I agreed to go down and look at the house. As usual, Jackson, in his Texan way, had exaggerated. The house was pleasant enough, with a view over the inland waterway, and just around the corner from Jackson's son, David, whom I'd never much liked, perhaps because he had encouraged Jackson in his philandering.

For several days, Jackson and I negotiated the possibility of my moving. Finally, I told him that one of the reasons I didn't want to move was because I didn't like the attitude of the Fort Lauderdale community, which had been founded to exclude Jewish residents. I didn't like the fact that black people could come there by day to work as servants and housekeepers, but that they weren't allowed on the streets after dark. I told him that if I moved there, I'd organize a campaign to allow blacks on the beach. After that, less was said about my moving.

The job of a legislator is not easy and I worked long hours to try to get bills passed, from a small item like the first Battle of Trenton stamp to protecting consumers from creditor errors, to conserving open space and exacting water pollution standards, to sponsoring the bill that allows voters to register by mail. It was a long time ago, but these initiatives and many more, I hope have had a lasting impact on the quality of people's lives here in New Jersey.

I visited the house in Fort Lauderdale from time to time. As time passed and I became more involved in my political work, I went down there less and less frequently. Jackson would eventually divorce me. By then, we were a married couple in name only. I threw myself into my work and I thought to myself, I was over sixty. It seemed to be too late for love to come to me.

Chapter Nine

1975 was a year of surprises. My duties in the Senate required long days, but the work was exhilarating. In February of that year, having had my usual medical checkup, I felt something was wrong in my intestine. I visited my doctor who pulled a long face and sent me for X–rays.

"I think you had better come in to see me," he said when he called me later.

He told me there was a growth, and he would have to operate.

"How soon?" I asked in trepidation.

"Next week."

In the recovery room, he came to tell me that there was a tumor, malignant although small, which had not invaded the intestinal wall. He removed twelve inches of my large intestine after a laparotomy. My doctor saw no reason for chemotherapy. In three weeks I was well enough to go to the Caribbean where the surgeon suggested swimming in salt water would hasten the healing process.

Mummy was not well herself. She had suffered several heart attacks. But she reserved her usual cottage at the Asticou Inn in North East Harbor, Maine. A few days before she planned to leave, she came into Princeton from her retirement home and had lunch at my house. Though she probably was not well enough to go to Maine, changing plans was always difficult for her. So she was driven up to Maine and one day later was in the hospital in Bar Harbor, stricken with a severe, almost fatal heart attack. I left the Senate for eight days to be there with her, and then flew her home in a chartered plane. My brother Blair came up too, and she made such a fuss about how wonderful it was for him to visit.

It was clear that she was very frail; her kidneys were beginning to fail. The doctor said he could send her to intensive care at the Princeton Hospital where she could live for six months on a dialysis machine. Remembering how deeply depressed she had been an earlier time in intensive care, we doubted if she could endure that. She had wanted to die, had increased her smoking to four packs a day—"a polite way to commit suicide," she told me during that last week. I was with her most of that final day. "Hold my hand," she said. Around noon she stopped breathing. It was very peaceful. It was the first time I'd been with someone when they died. And the peacefulness of her death has been a soothing thought since that day.

Mummy's funeral was held in Peapack at St. Luke's Church. She had planned every detail herself. She was buried, as she requested, at her mother's feet. My aunt Marise is buried at her mother's head. I miss her to this day and regret that her life was rarely happy.

*   *   *   *   *

Back in the Senate, I was studying the budget figures for the coming year in my office on State Street in Trenton when my secretary, Ethel, gave me a message from the governor's office.

"You're invited to the governor's mansion, 'Morven,' Sunday to meet Jimmy Carter, the governor of Georgia. All the legislators are invited."

"Jimmy who?"

"Jimmy Carter."

"Why do we want to meet Jimmy Carter?"

"He was governor of Georgia. Apparently he's running for President."

Although I did not know it yet, the invitation began my support and that of my brother Blair for the Carter candidacy, even though Blair had severe reservations at first. He had heard Carter speak on a number of occasions and thought that Carter's habit of so frequently mentioning his religion made him sound sanctimonious.

It was at the governor's mansion that I got my first glimpse of Jimmy Carter. He was not much taller than I, with a wide smile that was infectious. His face lit up when he spoke of the hopes that thousands of Americans had shared with him when he and Rosalyn had traveled around the country. During his campaign speeches, I found myself moved by his words and by his simple goodness, a sweetness in him and that he truly loved his neighbors and intended to do everything he could to make their lives better.

There were a number of candidates running in late 1975: Birch Bayh, Frank Church, Henry 'Scoop' Jackson, 'Mo' Udall and, always in the wings, Hubert Humphrey. No one in New Jersey was taking Carter seriously, except me. Members of our liberal group in New Jersey wanted to organize support for one candidate so as to have an impact on the Democratic Party as a whole.

"Let's get together and call ourselves something like The Committee for a Democratic Future," I told Dan Gaby, my friend from the New Democratic Coalition days.

"That's a good name," Dan said. "Do you think we could get Congressman Frank Thompson to chair the committee?"

"I'll ask him."

Thompy agreed to be chairman. We planned a late January meeting in my living room and about forty people came from around the state. Thompy opened the meeting.

"We're gathered here to discuss the candidates—Henry 'Scoop' Jackson, Birch Bayh, Frank Church, Jimmy Carter, and my colleague, Mo Udall. We liberals in the past have tended to split up rather than unite to support one candidate. This time we'll hear from those supporting each candidate, hold a straw vote—secret ballot, of course—and fall in behind whichever candidate has the most support."

Someone spoke up for Scoop Jackson; the arguments fell on deaf ears. Fred Bowen spoke eloquently for Udall.

"Any others?" Thompy said.

No one got up to speak. Ethel passed out slips of paper and then helped Thompy count the ballots once we had all voted.

"Thirty–nine for Mo Udall," Thompy said. "And one for Jimmy Carter."

"Who on earth could have voted for Jimmy Carter?" somebody wanted to know.

I did not confess.

In January 1976, the primaries began with caucus votes in Iowa. The Carters had personally visited one hundred and ten communities there, and Jimmy won a plurality of the delegates. Most political pundits were skeptical: "Jimmy who?" was a common refrain.

A month later Carter had a clear victory in New Hampshire. He then won solidly in Florida where his progressive record in civil rights earned him a majority of the state's black vote. He was able to win liberal votes in big cities for the same reason, and his country farmer background won support in smaller towns and rural areas.

I was encouraged by his success but too busy in the

Senate to contribute anything other than personal enthusiasm. Earlier, however, Patt Derian (wife of Hodding

Carter), who had known Jimmy Carter from their work together in the civil rights movement, had called and had come to New Jersey to talk about Carter's candidacy. She convinced me that it was important as a Northern liberal to announce public support of Carter, which would have the effect of countering criticisms in some camps that he was a zealot. So in April I did just that, sending my endorsement to the New Jersey papers and attending almost every campaign event in New Jersey.

It was mid–April, and the time for the decisive Pennsylvania primary was approaching. The *Chicago Daily News* called it High Noon: "There are 7 primaries down and 23 to go. It is a make or break proposition for Jimmy, Mo and Scoop (candidates with nicknames like that give contemporary politics an antic dimension)." The reporter went on to describe Carter's rise to eminence as "phenomenal," having no explanation for how a peanut farmer from the South had slipped into such fast company so quickly. Although President Ford's pardon of Nixon can also be considered a factor.

Carter won Pennsylvania on April 27. It was clear that he would win the nomination. I was jubilant.

The high point of the Democratic Convention that July, for me and perhaps millions of Americans, was the keynote address by Congresswoman Barbara Jordan. Her face shining with conviction and her voice ringing out in those measured cadences she was famous for, she began by reminding the assembly that Democrats have always stood for "equality for all, and privilege for none."

"We believe that the people are the source of all government power, that the authority of the people is to be extended, not restricted. We believe that the government has an obligation...to remove those obstacles which would block individual achievement, obstacles emanating from race, sex or economic conditions. Our belief is that the gap between the promise and reality of America can be closed. Many fear the future. Many are distrustful of their leaders, and believe their voices are never heard. Many seek to satisfy private wants, private interests. This is the great danger America faces. We (as public officials) must strike a balance between the idea that government should do everything…and the idea that government ought to do nothing."

She closed with a quote from Abraham Lincoln. "As I would not be a slave, so I would not be a master."

Granddaughter of slaves, Jordan captivated the convention and everyone in the country who was listening. And the danger she foresaw, "that private wants and private interests would prevail," was realized a short time later in the 1980s, and it is increasing daily.

Jimmy Carter was elected president in November of 1976. As a campaign contributor and organizer, I was invited to the inauguration. Inauguration Day was clear and very, very cold. I and my son George, along with his wife and children, shivered below the Capitol and then on the stands by the White House, watching Jimmy Carter take the oath of office. Toward the end of the Inaugural Parade, he and Rosalyn got out of the car, each holding one of daughter Amy's hands, to finish the march on foot.

George and I went to the reception at the White House. Jimmy gave me his usual hug when I went over to congratulate him, calling him "Mr. President." He corrected me. "Call me Jimmy," he said. President Carter illustrated the best qualities that exist in the American people, idealism, tolerance, persistence in following through on projects, humanity, and above all, love for all people.

I returned to Princeton after the festivities. The next day the telephone rang. It was Warren Christopher, the deputy secretary of state.

"I'm calling at the request of the president. He would like to appoint you to a new board. The board to review ambassadorial appointments."

"Thank you. What does that mean?"

"It means that non–career appointments will be reviewed and then recommendations made to the president."

"I am flattered, but may I think it over?" I wanted to check with a few people about whether or not this would be a good idea.

"If you hesitate because you might like to be an ambassador yourself, it would not be precluded." This really surprised me. I hadn't even thought about the possibility of becoming an ambassador.

I accepted the appointment to the board with excitement. At the second meeting of the Ambassadorial Review board, I ran into an old friend who was working at USAID in the hallway. "Anne," he said, "I have the perfect job for you: Director of the Office of Foreign Disaster Assistance (OFDA), a job that would allow you to help people in desperate need of assistance."

In May of 1977, I moved to Washington to take on the job as the National Director of Foreign Disaster Assistance and President Carter's Deputy Coordinator for International Disasters. My son George asked wryly, "You're in charge of Jimmy Carter's disasters?" Frank Wizner and his charming mother, Polly, my old school friend from St. Tim's, hosted an elegant reception to welcome me to Washington. Frank, a gifted career diplomat, was a helpful guide to a newcomer to the State Department.

The Office of U.S. Foreign Disaster Assistance (OFDA) was at that time responsible for directing and coordinating U.S. government relief assistance overseas. This office was within the USAID Bureau of Democracy, Conflict, and Humanitarian Assistance (DCHA). OFDA provided humanitarian assistance through mitigation and disaster response to rapid and slow onset disasters as well as complex emergencies.

In one year, 1977, the office provided assistance to 516 disasters in countries outside the United States. Since that time, OFDA relief has assuaged unimaginable human tragedies over the years—dealing with an estimated 3.6 million deaths and $18 billion worth of property damage. The aid was traditionally given in cooperation with private voluntary agencies like CARE and church organizations. I had a staff of nearly 30 extremely talented, experienced professionals who dedicated themselves, round the clock, to be of service to nations in need.

The Disaster Office was located on the first floor of the State Department. At one end was the situation room. On the other side, through glass windows, was a command post that received messages from any disaster area. In the center of this space was an oval table. It was a very imposing setup. At the time of a major foreign disaster, members of the staff, workers from other sections of the State Department, and Red Cross officials would be stationed around the table.

Each person had an assigned task, such as gathering supplies, coordinating logistics, setting up distribution channels, etc. At that time, there were then four regional disaster supply stockpiles in Guam, Singapore, Panama, and Italy—for medicine, food, tents, blankets, clothing, and other essentials. A staff member would arrange for military transport to deliver the necessary supplies to the disaster area.

The appropriate office in the Agency of International Assistance (AID) would arrange for food. The situation room would be in operation 24 hours a day until all was under control at the scene of the disaster.

The demands made on the Director of OFDA were complex. I had to run a program free of politics because my role was that of a humanitarian. Yet any mistakes made could have significant political ramifications. Therefore, we had to pay attention to both preparedness and relief programs. As the head of the United States government's international disaster relief, I knew I had to deal with the directors of other nations' relief agencies and go out in the field to assess for myself the effectiveness of our efforts.

By "our" I mean not only the work of the U.S. government but also voluntary agencies such as CARE, Catholic Relief Services, and Church World Services (a Protestant group). These organizations, as well as many smaller agencies, were the backbone of the U.S– International relief efforts. I had, and still have, the greatest admiration and respect for them. As the leader of an international program, I traveled to Geneva to meet with my international counterparts. In my meetings with them I stressed the American commitment to disaster preparedness and was impressed by certain governments, particularly the Scandinavians, who gave proportionately so much more to countries in need.

I traveled to the Sahel region in West Africa, to East Africa, to the Sudan and to Lebanon, as well as to the Caribbean to assess our relief work and to convey the message of preparedness and operational excellence. In India and Sri Lanka, I was appalled by the poverty and devastation suffered by hurricane and flood victims in the subcontinent. After a devastating tsunami there had flooded inland nine miles from the coastline, I was told that the men and children survived by climbing trees. The women wouldn't climb because of their saris and they drowned. An aide worker told me that in one village, nearly every woman was killed so he was asked to perform many quick weddings so that the children to have mothers.

I arrived in Sri Lanka shortly after they had suffered

a terrible hurricane and toured the island with the American
Ambassador. I could see firsthand the effect disaster relief
could have on a country that has few resources to begin with.
The Sri Lankans were kind and grateful. I was reminded of
my first trip to Guatemala, which was rebuilding after an
enormous earthquake where millions perished. As we drove
toward an affected area, in our big American car with flags
waving, there was a man picking flowers that would be sent
to florists to New York that evening. He came toward our car
and presented me with a huge bouquet of flowers and thanked
me and all Americans for our help. Today, with America's
reputation so damaged, I wonder if we would be greeted with
gratitude.

Yet, I was impressed by the resilience of the victims
as well as the compassion and professionalism of many
relief agencies and American governmental agencies. The
interrelated problems of war and famine continue today in
Rwanda and the Sudan, and in too many other places in the
world.

But one effort is now making a real difference. The
Carter Center, founded by Jimmy and Rosalynn Carter in
partnership with Emory University in Atlanta, is a nonprofit
and nongovernmental organization dedicated to fighting
disease, hunger, poverty, and conflict in developing countries.
The Center is one clear measure of Carter's global vision, and
its effectiveness hinges on much more than American "know—
how."

When Carter established the Center, he stressed the
importance of communicating directly with the country and
its citizens. The focus is on creating sustainable economies
and mobilizing the population on its own behalf. He said, "If,
for example, we want to increase agricultural productivity,
we go into the country and negotiate a written agreement,
a memorandum of understanding, with the president of the

nation. And we also require that the ministers of agriculture, education, health, and transportation all become involved. And let's say we start out with 40 farmers the first year, scattered around the country, then their neighbors can watch to see how much benefit they can derive from using a few simple principles like contour planting and moderate amounts of fertilizer. It's really a matter of one farmer letting another see the advantage. It's the power of example."

When Jimmy Carter received the Nobel Peace Prize in 2002, he underscored the mission of the Carter Center in his acceptance speech: "Most work of The Carter Center is in remote villages in the poorest nations of Africa, and there I have witnessed the capacity of destitute people to persevere under heartbreaking conditions. I have come to admire their judgment and wisdom, their courage and faith, and their awesome accomplishments when given a chance to use their innate abilities. But tragically, in the industrialized world there is a terrible absence of understanding or concern about those who are enduring lives of despair and hopelessness. We have not yet made the commitment to share with others an appreciable part of our excessive wealth. This is a potentially rewarding burden that we should all be willing to assume... The bond of our common humanity is stronger than the divisiveness of our fears and prejudices. God gives us the capacity for choice. We can choose to alleviate suffering. We can choose to work together for peace. We can make these changes – and we must."

Perhaps war and famine can eventually be eliminated. Until then, relief organizations such as OFDA play a critical role. They keep people alive, and they keep the conscience of the world focused on terrible human suffering. I will not soon forget the fractured buildings in Guatemala City, the flooded delta of Andra Pradesh, the streets of Calcutta so crowded with the poor and homeless that they seemed like so many

pebbles in the sea. My work with OFDA sharpened my sense of an international community and made me more acutely aware of the responsibilities we have not only as American citizens but as citizens of the world.

* * * * *

One early spring morning in 1979, the courtyard at my home in Kalorama Square in Washington, D.C. was blooming with crocuses and daffodils under the small, young oak trees. I was at my desk, enjoying the spring sunshine and watching my neighbors come and go. Senator Bentsen lived to my right, *Washington Post* editorial writer Philip Geyelin and his wife were on my left, and across the courtyard, was The *New York Times* columnist Scotty Reston and his wife Sally. They had shown me every kindness since I moved to Kalorama Square. Since I traveled frequently as with Disaster Relief Office, it was comforting to be surrounded by so many dear friends.

On the occasional summer evening when I was home, I would float in the pool, quiet and alone. I would look around and observe my neighbors' dinner parties and occasionally recognize the political figures, diplomats and journalists who were their guests. I was sometimes invited to these parties, but it was just as entertaining to observe them unseen. I thought sometimes of writing a play called "Kalorama Square" with this splendid cast of characters.

One quiet Saturday morning I got a call from Carol Laise who had taken my place on the Presidential Advisory Board on Ambassadorial Appointments, which reviewed nominees' qualifications and made recommendations to the president.

"There are three ambassadorial vacancies coming up," she said. "Would you be interested?"

"Where are they?" I answered.

"Canada, Sri Lanka, and New Zealand."

Although I would have loved to go back up to Canada, everything I had heard about New Zealand appealed to me, from its green and lovely landscape, to its important role in United States foreign policy. Their diplomatic corps had a wonderful reputation. I quickly did some research and learned that New Zealand had a population of three million people and sixty–three million sheep. They had then and still have a parliamentary system of government, and a Prime Minister is elected every three years.

In 2008, they are one of the few countries in the world with a woman Prime Minister. After World War II, New Zealand began to enjoy autonomy from Britain. From that point, until after my tenure as Ambassador, it had aligned itself diplomatically as a close friend of the United States. As a democracy that shares a similar hope and vision for the future, New Zealand has supported peacekeeping and economic developments that promote world harmony and prosperity. I was certain this was the appointment I would most welcome. So I agreed that Carol should put my name before the Ambassadorial Board for an appointment to New Zealand.

Carol's next call came sooner than expected, just a few weeks later.

"The secretary of state, the head of the National Security Council, and the President have met and approved your appointment—it's being sent to the Senate for confirmation."

I literally jumped for joy. I called my children and my friends. I thought how pleased my mother would have been. Had she been alive, I would have invited her to go with me. How she would have enjoyed saying, "My daughter, the Ambassador."

A few days later, my briefings for the post began. Frank Bennett, the desk officer in charge of Australia and New Zealand, gave me books to read. Because policy statements were discussed between the State Department and its American embassies through the exchange of cables, I also looked over the cable traffic to study the communications between the embassy in Wellington and Washington.

"Is Muldoon still the Prime Minister? " I asked Frank Bennett.

"Yes. His party, the National Party, is more conservative than the other major party, the Labor Party. Assistant Secretary of State Dick Holbrooke is going to want you to get to know members of the Labor party. Your predecessor discouraged any contact with them. He regarded them as Communists."

"He must have been a right–winger," I said.

"He was a good ambassador in many ways, but he did have his prejudices," said Frank.

In June, Merv Norish, the New Zealand Ambassador to the United States, gave a dinner party at his residence in Washington. At dinner I was seated on the right of Prime Minister Muldoon, who seemed ill at ease. My first impression of him was that he looked like a bulldog. He was a little shorter than I was with a girth almost as wide as his shoulders.

I assumed politics might provide a topic of mutual interest.

"I used to be in the New Jersey legislature," I said. "We would have had an easier time if ours had been a unicameral legislature like yours." Prime Minister Muldoon looked off into space.

"I do not like 'lady' politicians," he said.

End of conversation.

I retold this story to a reporter, off the record, but he

published it anyway. I got in a bit of hot water right off the bat, but at least they knew I had a sense of humor.

My confirmation hearings were held before the Senate Foreign Relations Committee on June 26. Despite the image of Prime Minister Muldoon playing in my head, I closed my statement with this declaration: "I feel that I am going to paradise."

When I stepped off the airplane in Wellington as the new American Ambassador to New Zealand, the press peppered me with questions. This time I made a point of being very polite and definitely not funny.

Chapter Ten

Soon after my confirmation, I was invited, as an observer, to attend the ANZUS Pact meeting. This was a security arrangement between the United States, Australia, and New Zealand formed at Australia and New Zealand's request in the early 1950s. The Australia, New Zealand, United States Security Treaty (ANZUS or ANZUS Treaty) came about following the close cooperation of the United States, Australia, and New Zealand during World War II, during which time Australia had come perilously close to invasion by Japan. Following the end of World War II, the United States was eager to normalize relations with Japan, particularly as the Korean War was still raging a short distance from Japan. With the involvement of China and possibly the Soviet Union in Korea, the Cold War was threatening to become a full scale war. However, Australia and New Zealand in particular were extremely reluctant to finalize a peace treaty with Japan that would allow for Japanese rearmament. Both countries relented only when an Australian and New Zealand proposal for a three way security treaty was accepted by the United States.

The resulting treaty concluded in San Francisco on September 1st, 1951, and entered into force on April 29th, 1952. The treaty bound the signatories to recognize that an armed attack in the Pacific on any of them would endanger the peace and safety of the others. It stated: "The parties will consult together whenever in the opinion of any of them the territorial integrity, political independence or security of any of the parties is threatened in the Pacific." The three nations also pledged to maintain and develop individual and collective capabilities to resist attack.

These initial ANZUS meetings were very helpful in enlarging my understanding of the military and security arrangements in the South Pacific.

On the way back to Washington I made a brief, unofficial stop in New Zealand to meet my deputy and take a look at the residence so that I would know what furniture and personal items to send out.

Joe Breen, the embassy chauffeur, met me and my friend Nancy Muir, who had flown out to meet me. She had often helped me with decorating and had come for that purpose. Joe was to drive me to the Ambassadorial residence, but he first showed us the spectacular Wellington Harbor.

"I think of Joe as my best friend," former Ambassador Selden's wife had told me when I saw her in Washington. "He immigrated to New Zealand from London, you know, in 1974. Every Ambassador since then has felt that it would be hard to function effectively without him."

Joe rang the bell after we drove up to the tree–shaded driveway, bordered by camellia bushes. Tio, the Malaysian butler, answered the door. Joe introduced us to him and Awa, his wife, who was the cook.

"Awa, Tio, this is the new Ambassador designate. Will you show her the house?"

We started downstairs, in the large, blue–carpeted living room that looked as though it belonged in an upscale motel. But in spite of that, I felt right at home. I could picture in my mind living in that house, entertaining members of the government and important visitors from the United States. I could imagine bringing pieces of my own furniture.

Our tour of the residence continued as we looked at the dining room that was on the left of the entrance door.

"This is a very nice room with its blue rug and yellow

and blue curtains," I said, "but it looks small, as if it could not seat more than twelve people."

"We can get eighteen seated at small tables, Madam," Joe said. "But a few years ago a room called the Pavilion was added. It's down this way." Joe led us down a passage and we saw a big room, comfortably furnished, with lots of windows.

"We can seat thirty–six people here. Ambassador Selden entertained here once every three weeks."

I heard a rumor later that my predecessor ordered far more food than necessary for his family and guests and used the leftovers for the next three weeks. The U.S. government pays for food used for entertaining New Zealanders, but not for food for personal family use.

"Let's go upstairs," Nancy said. On the second floor we found four bedrooms and three baths. When we came down again, Awa showed us the spacious kitchen, with two large refrigerators and a restaurant style stove.

"I'll show you the garden," Joe said. "This property was once part of a famous public garden. The trees are big and old. At the end of the lawn is a rose garden. Some ambassadors have complained that the residence wasn't grand enough."

"Goodness," I said. "It's lovely, comfortable, and gracious. Somehow I don't believe that it would be right to have an elaborate mansion in New Zealand."

"That's right," Joe said. "It's really not done to have a grand house. They call it 'flash' here; it might be resented."

*   *   *   *   *

In mid–July I was back in Washington where Vice President Mondale swore me in, in his office. All my children and several grandchildren came to the ceremony. My twelve–

year–old granddaughter, Katie Luther, held my great–grandmother Blair's Bible.

My briefings were over, the house in Kalorama Square sublet, my goods and chattels packed and shipped. And so, in mid–August of 1979, I set out on my great adventure: I was the United States "Ambassador Extraordinary and Plenipotentiary" to New Zealand. My son George arrived with me and stayed three weeks, partly to do research on our relative John Ledyard, who had been in New Zealand in 1777 with Captain Cook.

*   *   *   *   *

I ARRIVED AT 6:15 AM AUGUST 22, 1979, AND TOOK CHARGE OF THE POST. One hour after I landed in Wellington, I sent the customary cable that ambassadors use to notify the State Department of their arrival.

It was mid–winter, scarcely light, and very cold. My deputy, Terry Healy, whom I inherited from my predecessor, was at the foot of the airplane steps. She was an old–fashioned Foreign Service officer who believed in following antiquated customs. The entire American staff, nearly thirty strong, were lined up behind her. They looked as if they were prepared to salute. At one time, when an ambassador arrived or left the country, it had been the custom to have the entire staff on hand. I had not expected it. I was touched and a little embarrassed. I felt warmly welcomed but wished they had not been ordered to turn out on such a cold, dark winter's morning.

The press was also out in force. That I did expect since I was New Zealand's first woman ambassador from any country.

"How will you get on with the Prime Minister?" the

reporters asked. I knew now how to answer these questions diplomatically.

"Very well, I expect. He's an intelligent man and a great friend of the United States."

"But he's said he didn't like lady politicians."

"Oh, that was a silly story," I replied.

Joe drove me and my son George, who had flown out with me, to Lower Hutt in the big black car with the flags flying from the front fenders.

"This is really exciting," George said.

"It's good to have you here, to share the excitement with me."

As we drove into the town, we passed a greengrocer.

"Oh, George, just look at that display of fruits and vegetables. I wish we could stop right now and get out my paints – the greens of the lettuce, the yellows of lemons and oranges, the reds of the apples…"

"I'll stop the car, Madam, if you wish," Joe said.

"No, no, Joe. I'll do that another day."

We drove on toward the residence. There was a school nearby and some of the children were gathering near it.

"Do your daughters go there?" I asked Joe.

"No, we live on the other side of Wellington."

"The children look so happy!" Some months later my friends, Walter and Leo Clark, who had founded North Country School in the Adirondacks where Roger had gone as a boy, came to visit. They too were struck by the openness and cheerfulness of the children of New Zealand.

I stayed at the residence the first day, resting and unpacking. And then, quickly, it was time to get acquainted and get down to business.

The next morning I went to the chancery to meet with my deputy, the senior officers, the political and economic advisors. They briefed me on the political situation, urging me to befriend members of the Labor Party (branded by my predecessor as "Communists") and confirmed what I already suspected, that Prime Minister Muldoon and I would not become fast friends.

I met with the CIA station chief and was taken into the communication room, a secure space where conversations could not be bugged. Wrapped in what looked like tinfoil, the room made me feel claustrophobic.

There had been rumors of CIA interference during previous elections in New Zealand and Australia. Once I got to know the members of the Labor Party, they assured me there had been no interference in New Zealand. The CIA was monitoring the peace movement and antinuclear groups, and the "Communists" in New Zealand—all three of them.

After the tour I sat at my desk, glancing out the window at Wellington, the capital city. I felt the weight of the responsibility I had taken on. I did not want to let my country down or disappoint my President. But I was also excited: This was my kind of country, beautiful and green, where there was real concern about the environment and conservation, two of my major interests. The Prime Minister was something of a problem, but I thought I could handle it. He was not popular, though I knew the Prime Minister was a very powerful position in New Zealand and Robert Muldoon was a master politician.

I was to discover quickly what sorts of issues Robert Muldoon liked to manipulate. Our nuclear Navy was one such target. Our ships, given the mandate of patrolling the Pacific from California right through the coast of Africa, were nuclear powered. U.S. policy was to neither confirm nor deny their nuclear capability. The nuclear powered engines on each ship were carefully shielded, the crews meticulously trained in safety procedures. Nonetheless, when one of our ships came into New Zealand ports, protesters in sailboats, motorboats, and rowboats circled it and hampered its safe passage. I was told that Muldoon deliberately exploited the issue, announcing the visit of a U.S. ship well in advance of its arrival, giving the protesters plenty of time to organize. The police were then ordered to arrest them. No wonder the peace movement grew so strong in New Zealand.

* * * * *

CLUB ENTITLED NOT TO ADMIT TOP WOMAN!

So ran the headline in the Wellington Dominion soon after my arrival. The news story spelled it out: "Ambassador Martindell will not be permitted to become a member of the influential men–only Wellington Club."

If the story proved true, I would be the first American ambassador not to allowed to be a member of the 139–year–old club. Rumor had it that all important decisions about New Zealand, whether political or economic, were made there. All my male diplomatic colleagues were invited to join, as were the male members of my staff. The club's 850 members included all the leading businessmen and politicians in New Zealand.

"I haven't applied," I told my deputy right after reading the article. "So what is all this about?"

"You shouldn't apply, ambassador," Terry said. "The Canadian high commissioner, Irene Johnson, did apply, and the membership board asked her deputy to persuade her to withdraw her name 'to save the club embarrassment.'"

The following day a journalist asked the club secretary about membership for Irene and me. His answer was, "Why, they can just ask one of their male staff to arrange use of the club occasionally."

The club policy would not change until twelve years after my departure. A later club president told me how it came about. A woman was made a judge, the first in New Zealand, and all judges as well as all ambassadors were automatically invited. He took up her cause.

"I had a bloody fight, but I won. She's a member, and there are a few more women now."

One of the headlines before I arrived had my picture on the front page – over large letters that read "GRANAMBASSADOR."

"Plenty of male ambassadors have had grandchildren," my aunt Marise pointed out after I sent her a copy.

"They haven't inspired headlines," I said.

My son George left to return to his family in Seattle, where later he would found a sister city organized with Seattle and Christchurch. My eighty year old aunt—Marise Campbell, my mother's youngest sister—arrived in mid–September. She swung off the plane from Australia in a fashionable red suit. She took charge of the house and its two–and–a–half acre garden. She had played the maternal role in my life from time to time and was doing so again. My children called her "Auntie Mame."

It didn't take long for Marise, a 1920s glamour girl, once the toast of Paris and New York, to become the "Belle of Wellington." And a local newspaper ran an article under the headline "You're a Tonic, Mrs. Campbell," the article read in part: "The greatest tonic for rejuvenating lagging 40, 50, 60 and 70 olds may be a half–hour spent talking with 80–year–old Mrs. Blair Campbell. If you're tired with life, perhaps you can capture an ounce or two of her effervescence...

"Sitting poised, with large sunglasses and just an hour or two out of a beauty salon, Mrs. Campbell gives the impression that over the years she might have talked a lot of people into doing what she wanted....

"Like the slogan of a well–known beverage: 'She's still going strong.' Oh – and by the way, she likes whisky."

I told Marise about a week after she arrived that since I was also ambassador to Western Samoa I needed to visit and present my credentials as soon as possible. My aunt astonished Joe by renting a car and driving herself around to make several visits to friends of friends while I was away. At a dinner party in Wellington early in September, Marise and I had met the Prime Minister of Western Samoa, Efi Tupuola," a very fine–looking man," as Marise described him. Certainly he was charming and cordial, providing me with quite a different reception from Prime Minister Muldoon's.

On arrival at Apia, West Samoa, I found the economic officer, Dick Imus; his wife Illa; the Peace Corps director, Carolyn Gulat; and our consular agent Vernon McKenzie, a Samoan, waiting at the foot of the airplane steps. In accordance with Polynesian custom, they wreathed me with dozens of fragrant garlands and took me to Aggie Grey's Hotel on the waterfront.

When Gauguin first saw Tahiti, he must have seen something very much like Western Samoa – lush, green, sleepy, with lovely bays and beaches, and delectable young women, known as wahini. As we drove along the coast, each turn of the road revealed a new cove, coral beach, or rocky outcrop.

The next day we rose at six to climb in the cool of the morning, through the tropical forest and up a very steep trail to the summit of Mt. Vaea to visit the grave of Robert Lewis Stevenson, one of my favorite poets.

As we climbed, I learned that Stevenson – whom the Samoans called "Tusitala" or "Teller of Tales" – was much beloved. After a few years in Samoa, he lost his long fight to tuberculosis and died following a stroke. When word went

out to the chiefs, they marshaled their men and by the light
of torches hacked all night to cut the trail to the top of the
mountain. As we climbed, I was told Stevenson breathed
his last breath in the early morning hours of December 3,
1894. He was placed in his coffin, and chiefs carried it on
their shoulders to the heights and reverently buried him in
the grave they had dug. The stone that marks his grave is
inscribed with some of his verse:

> Here he lies where he longed to be;
> Home is the sailor, home from the sea,
> And the hunter, home from the hill.

As I read these words, I thought, there lies Robert
Louis Stevenson, who grew up in the gray Scottish city of
Edinburgh. He wrote that as a small boy he used to press his
nose against a cold windowpane and watch "Auld Leekie" light
the street lamps in the dark afternoons. Now he lies where one
can look out on the blue Pacific as it rolls to a shore dotted
with palm trees. The sun shines there every day.

The Polynesians always seem to be feasting. Roast
pig, a favorite dish, is cooked in an oven dug underground.
I would be as large as the Royal Family of Tonga if I had
been in residence in Apia instead of New Zealand. After one
such feast, Aggie Grey, the hotel owner, told me about her
friendship with the queen of Tonga, Queen Salote. The Queen
weighed several hundred pounds and her bulk filled an entire
carriage at Queen Elizabeth II's coronation. Aggie said she
often visited Queen Salote and that her ladies in waiting
could only approach Her Majesty on their knees. Her son, the
present king, was well over six feet tall and weighed between
three and four hundred pounds.

My Aunt Marise, who met the King in Wellington, said
he looked like a turtle standing up – and he indeed had a small

head on top of a huge body. When he traveled by air to the Chatham Islands, he chartered a plane large enough to carry his enormous bed, which always went with him.

The king went to New York City for a medical check–up and the doctor told him that he would have to lose weight. What, the doctor asked him, was his usual diet? The king replied that it was taro, a Polynesian starchy root vegetable.

"Well," said the doctor, "don't eat more than one a day." The average taro weighs about ten pounds.

I visited American Samoa several times on the way to or from Western Samoa. Peter Coleman, the governor, was charming, intelligent, and very knowledgeable about Western Samoa and all of the South Pacific. Because American Samoa received television signals from America and beamed them to Western Samoa, Governor Coleman was better known in Western Samoa than their own Prime Minister.

He introduced me to the President of the Senate and the Speaker of the House of American Samoa. Their legislature was modeled on ours, while Western Samoa's was modeled on New Zealand's unicameral body. In Western Samoa only the Matai, the one thousand hereditary nobles, could vote. This electoral system changed in 1990, when universal suffrage was voted in by a narrow margin.

The American Samoan President of the Senate and the Speaker of the House invited me to lunch. When they met me, they were dressed in high Samoan style: pastel blue lava–lavas (kilted skirts ending at the knees), shirts and ties, and bare feet. After touring the building where the legislature sat, we went to a Chinese restaurant.

As soon as we had ordered our lunch, the Speaker turned to me and said, "Where can I find Margaret Mead?"

"You'll have to ascend to heaven. She died recently."

Margaret Mead was a heroine of mine – but was not, apparently, of the Speaker's.

"I would have liked to kill her," he proclaimed.

"Why?"

"You know that as a young woman she came out here to study our customs. We were hospitable. My mother asked her to stay with our family. She could speak no Samoan, so some young women translated for her in her interviews. The women found her young and naïve, so they amused themselves by making up stories about the sexual customs of our young people. Her book, Coming of Age in Samoa, caused a sensation—and it gave our young girls a bad name."

Though I've never researched the veracity of Mead's account, I did wonder whether it was indeed as accurate as it was portrayed in our country. My own observations led me to conclude that Samoans had strict standards for their children.

The plane back to Wellington was delayed by an airline strike so I had to return by way of Fiji. I was delighted to do so because I got to see Suva, to meet Robert Craig, the AID director for the area, and to dine with Ambassador Condon.

When I told Bob Craig about the feasting in Apia, he said he would never forget being invited to one of the outer Polynesian islands of Fiji for a feast.

"I expected roast pig or at least delicious fish," he said. "So you can imagine my surprise when they proudly brought out a can of corned beef. 'Pisuppo,' they proudly called it, which sounded an awful lot like pea soup."

The missionaries, who insisted that the Polynesian maidens cover up their beautiful breasts with ugly cotton shifts, had encouraged a canned diet. All cans were therefore known as "pisuppo."

The Ambassador told a story of a British Ambassador late in the last century who was sailing to take up his post somewhere in the Pacific. He sent word that he would be bringing his nineteen year old daughter with him. In deference to her Victorian sensibilities, he asked if the young ladies, who always met the ships, would cover their breasts for his daughter's arrival. They did so, but they bared their beautiful round bottoms instead!

*   *   *   *   *

One day in 1980, Dick Dols, the political officer, came to see me about a proposed trip to the Tokelau Islands, three tiny atolls, to sign a treaty.

"Ambassador, there have been negotiations going on for some years about several islands, twenty–six all told. The United States has laid claim to them."

"How did that happen?"

"A ship Captain, crossing the Pacific, would see an island, chart it on the map, and say, 'That island belongs to the United States,' often without even landing on it."

"Really, how amazing!"

"Yes, but in 1980, we gave up our claims to all but one, called Swain's Island, near American Samoa. A family by the name of Jennings lived there and grew pineapples. No one lives there now."

"That's interesting, my grandmother Blair's maiden name was Jennings. Her grandfather was a ship Captain. I wonder if he stopped there and found a Polynesian bride – so to speak."

"In any case, as the Tokelau Islands are a protectorate of New Zealand, Foreign Affairs would like you to go up there and sign the treaty, which will renounce all but Swain's Island."

"Where are they and how would I get there, Dick?"

"The three tiny islands, which are coral atolls surrounding a lagoon, are a day's sail from Western Samoa. They have been discussing how to get you there as only one rusty old ship goes once a month with mail and supplies. They feel it is not suitable for the American Ambassador's travel, so they've arranged that a frigate from the Royal New Zealand Navy will be able to pick you up in Western Samoa. Frank Corner, the permanent head of Foreign Affairs, will accompany you, and I will go also."

On November 29, 1980, we flew to Western Samoa and boarded the ship Otago.

The Captain greeted me as I boarded.

"Welcome, Ambassador. I have given up my cabin so you may sleep there; I'll take you to it now."

"But Captain, you did not need to do that. I do not want to disturb you."

"Well, I have the only private plumbing. We could not have you sharing the head with the men."

The cabin was small but comfortable.

The Captain said, "The only other lady who has come on board was Princess Margaret. The sheets on the bunk were the ones we used for her." His tone indicated that I had been honored. I wondered, had they been washed?

The night was rather rough, but I slept well. The evening before, Frank Corner said, "We'll be stopping at the first island about six tomorrow morning to pick up the chief, the Faipule, and his entourage. It is not necessary for you to be on deck to greet the chief."

"Of course I'll be there."

I welcomed the Faipule and his seventeen ladies and other officials shortly after six.

"It is on this island," said Frank, *sotto voce*, "that you see the fishing pigs."

"What do you mean?" I asked.

"Pigs literally go out on the rocks and find shellfish, crack the shells with their hooves, and eat the fish. I've seen them."

We stopped at the second island to pick up their delegation and then cruised to Atafu, with fifty–eight Tokoloans on board, where the signing was to take place. We arrived there about nine in the morning.

"Anne," Frank said, "the ship will anchor off shore. The only way to land, as there is no dock, is to go through the surf in a zodiak (a rubber boat). Don't worry about it, though. The strong men of the island will go out into the water waist deep and hold and guide the boat in. You won't have to ride the waves."

The sea was very rough that day. The Captain sent the communications team with their radar equipment to shore so we on the ship could communicate with the chiefs and their council. Their boat overturned, but somehow they landed with enough functional equipment. They sent back word that it was too rough, and that I should not come through the surf. There were endless consultations by radio between Frank Corner, the chiefs from the other islands on the ship Otago and the Faipule of Atafu. I heard Frank Corner suggest it would be possible to declare the ship's deck Tokelau territory, invite the Atafu chief and his council aboard and sign the treaty there.

When this was relayed by radio to Atafu, the airwaves crackled. That arrangement did not suit them at all. They refused to come aboard the ship; we must come to them. There were lengthy discussions by radio. After two hours of arguments, Frank Corner said to the assembled company on the Captain's bridge, two chiefs, two council men and me, "I don't care what you decide, but decide now."

"Yes," the Captain said to the radio operator, "relay Mr. Corner's statement to the chief and council on Atafu. The sea is getting rougher. I won't be responsible for the ambassador's safety."

Finally the Faipule in Atafu won. We were to go on

shore. I stood at the top of the ladder hanging over the ship's side, in trousers, carrying my dress. The officer standing ready to help me down said, "By the way, Madam Ambassador, can you swim?"

"Yes, but suppose I said I couldn't? I see you're not giving me a life jacket." I climbed down the ladder to the little boat tossing below. The sailors rowed us toward the shore. The strong island men grabbed the boat as it approached the surf pounding the beach. We made it in without overturning.

We crossed the beach to a palm grove, where a path led to a large wooden building. The paths were raked as carefully as a Japanese garden. Beautifully woven baskets hung from the palm trees, just as one would hang ornaments on a Christmas tree.

"Oh, Dick," I said. "I'm glad we decided to land. They must have spent weeks getting ready."

"You can slip into this building to change," Dick said.

The crowd gathered by the big building. Frank Corner spoke. I gave my prepared speech, which was translated. Then the old chief from the first island rose. I was told that he complained that I spoke too long; it cut into his time. He said they were not happy that they had to give up Swain's Island; it was larger than the three Tokelan atolls put together. After several more speeches, which lasted an hour, we signed the treaty. After the formalities, there was a Polynesian feast with roast pig, of course, and other delicacies. The pig tasted fishy.

"Mr. Corner," one of the communications crew said, "I've a message from the Captain. He sees a very large storm on his radar. It is approaching rapidly. You must get the ambassador back to the ship at once."

There is no such thing as "at once" in Polynesia. The Tokalauans were dismayed they had to shorten the speeches and toasts. It was an hour before we could go to the little boat on the beach. The strong men holding the boat got us through the surf. We approached the ship.

"Goodness, Frank," I said. "Those swells must be nine to eleven feet; the frigate is tossing wildly."

"We'll fix a platform for you with a couple of fishing boats that are higher than the zodiak. They say you can walk across them to the ship's side."

"And then jump to the ladder in this sea? Wow!" I said, feeling queasy.

As I stood on the deck of the wooden fishing boat, the ladder seemed a mile away.

An officer called from the deck. "Ambassador, when I say jump, you jump."

"Jump," he yelled. Out of the corner of my eye, I saw a huge wave coming on my right. It looked like the Alaskan tidal wave I saw in a film shown in the Foreign Disaster Office. I stepped back. The wave lifted the little wooden boat and smashed it into the side of the frigate. The sound of cracking wood was deafening. If I had not stepped back, I might have broken both legs. There was no doctor on board. We were twelve hours away from Apia and days away from New Zealand.

There was a slight lull.

"Jump," yelled the officer. I jumped to the ladder, catching hold with one foot and one hand. Shaking, I climbed to the deck.

"Thank God, Ambassador," the Captain said, as he gave me a hand over the rail. "You are in one piece." His face was pale. "I don't know how I would have explained it if anything had happened to you."

"Oh, I'm fine. It was an adventure," I said with false enthusiasm. I was 64 years old at the time.

Wet and shaken, I returned to the cabin to change into dry clothes. Then I returned to the bridge. Frank Corner and the Captain were there. We were proceeding toward the other two small islands. The ship was rising and falling in the big swells.

Frank said, "There is a big feast prepared at each of the islands. We'll go ashore to celebrate with them."

"Do I have to go in the rubber Zodiak boat to land on those islands?"

"Yes. It's up to you whether you go. I'll have to go anyway."

"Then the American Ambassador will go also."

Chapter Eleven

"Mr. Malcolm Ott, the American consular agent in Christchurch, is calling," my secretary announced.

"Put him on, please," I said.

"Ambassador, may I offer my congratulations?" he said. "My wife and I are looking forward to seeing you. I'm calling because every October the American Navy sends a contingent, some nine hundred strong, down to the Antarctic for the summer. They hope you'll come to Christchurch for the farewell service before they leave for 'the Ice,' as they call McMurdo Base in Antarctica."

"I'd like to come. Thank you."

"Good. Then you can see Operation Deep Freeze, as well. Every year the ambassador is asked to make an address at the Christchurch Cathedral at this time—would you be willing to do that?"

"I'd be glad to," I said. I rarely turn down an invitation to speak!

Malcolm Ott sighed with obvious relief. "That's wonderful. Ambassadors are always asked to make the address for the farewell service, but you're the first one to accept."

Joe drove me to the Cathedral in the Embassy Lincoln Continental, flags flying from the fenders. We approached slowly, ceremoniously. My 80 year old aunt was on the sidewalk, camera in hand. She later wrote in one of her "dearest family" letters: "I walked around the corner from the hotel to the big Christchurch Cathedral so I could photograph Anne sweeping up in that big black car. The bishop in his white cope and mitre and the dean in a scarlet robe stood

waiting to escort her. On the way into the Cathedral they
passed the guard of honor, who saluted, and were followed by
our entire naval contingent in their blues. I know exactly how
Prince Philip feels as I am learning to walk three paces behind
Anne and to let her go through the doors first. Anne and I sat
alone in the front pew with the Navy behind us."

This service to bless the Navy and the scientists going to
the Antarctic for the summer season is an annual occurrence.
The New Zealanders who go to the nearby Scott base on the
Ross Ice Shelf are blessed as well. They sang that familiar
robust hymn, "Eternal Father, Strong to Save:"

Eternal Father, Strong to save,
Whose arm hath bound the restless wave,
Who bid'st the mighty Ocean deep
Its own appointed limits keep;
O hear us when we cry to thee,
for those in peril on the sea.

O Christ! Whose voice the waters heard
And hushed their raging at Thy word,
Who walked'st on the foaming deep,
and calm amidst its rage didst sleep;
Oh hear us when we cry to Thee
For those in peril on the sea!

Most Holy spirit! Who didst brood
Upon the chaos dark and rude,
And bid its angry tumult cease,
And give, for wild confusion, peace;

Oh, hear us when we cry to Thee
For those in peril on the sea!

O Trinity of love and power!
Our brethren shield in danger's hour;
From rock and tempest, fire and foe,
Protect them wheresoe'er they go;
Thus evermore shall rise to Thee,
Glad hymns of praise from land and sea.

I recall that the ceremony included a startling moment when there was a sudden flash behind me. Turning slightly, I saw a photographer crouching behind me. It occurred to me that he could have been holding a gun rather than a camera.

In my address I quoted Genesis: "Let the waters under the heavens be gathered into one place and let the dry land appear." I told them that scientists believe there was originally one landmass that later separated into seven continents. Antarctica, the seventh, was discovered last. I also told them about the elegant Greek theory of bilateral symmetry in us and in nature. Since the Phoenicians who sailed north of Britain reported finding "great mountains of ice," the Greeks reasoned that there must be a similar mass in the south. In my speech I also referred to the Antarctic Treaty, which had been renewed before I came to New Zealand, as a landmark of international cooperation.

After the service we lunched with the Dean of the Cathedral. Then that night we went to Base Commander Cranz's house.

"Welcome, Ambassador," he said. "This is a farewell party for the men and the woman who are going 'south.' I have to stay here in Christchurch to see that supplies leave every other day for the next four to five months until they return. Flights have to go while there's daylight down there. In the total darkness of winter we send an occasional mail drop, and we have to be sure that we'll have ten hours of decent weather for the roundtrip."

"I understand that the winds howl around the pole in the winter," I said. "How many people will winter over at McMurdo this year?"

"Altogether there'll be thirty—eight men, one woman, and a dog. The men are all scientists, and the woman is the doctor. Nine of them will be at the pole."

At eight the next morning, Aunt Marise and I went to the base in the pouring rain to wave the sailors goodbye. The officers gave us big hugs.

"We'll see you on the ice before Christmas," Captain Westbrook said.

"Aren't you glad you have a lady ambassador you can kiss?" Marise said.

Captain Westbrook approached the huge Starlifter plane that would fly them south. "I expect to be in McMurdo at three in the afternoon," he said. "There will be sunshine there, I'm told." He climbed the steps to enter the plane, pausing at the top for a final wave, tall, blond, and blue—eyed in his becoming Navy blues. He was very good—looking.

Captain Westbrook had come to call on me in Wellington, in September, soon after his arrival in Christchurch to prepare for his assignment in Antarctica.

After the usual pleasantries, he became serious.

"Madame Ambassador, I wish you would convey to the New Zealand government that the tourist flights by Air New Zealand to the Antarctic are courting danger. They do not land. They're supposed to stay well above the height of Mt. Erebus, which is ten thousand feet high. But they often fly much lower so the passengers can see the glaciers and terrain. We lack the communications equipment to monitor them properly or to guide them. If there should be an accident I would have to send my men to their rescue, thereby endangering them. Please carry this message to the highest level."

I made an appointment with the Prime Minister and saw him a few days later.

"Prime minister," I said. "I'm here at the request of the American Navy Captain in charge of the McMurdo base in the Antarctic."

"Yes, Ambassador, what does he want?"

"To put it bluntly, he feels that the tourist flights of Air New Zealand and the Australian airline Qantas are dangerous. They have been asked to fly higher than Mt. Erebus, but often they don't. Apparently they want to give the tourists a better view. The Navy doesn't have the proper equipment to guide them; that's not their job. He hopes— and I hope—that you'll persuade them to discontinue these tourist flights. I'm sure no one wants an accident." I described the hazards as Captain Westbrook had explained them to me.

"Ambassador, I will discuss it with the Air New Zealand officials," the Prime Minister said when I finished. He dismissed me with a wave of his hand.

It seemed as if the Prime Minister was not taking the warning seriously. At that time the New Zealand government wholly owned Air New Zealand, and the president of the airline was a close friend of Prime Minister Muldoon. The tourist flights continued with planes filled with families in summer clothes out for a lark. The Prime Minister never gave me the courtesy of a reply.

In the embassy, we were pleased when high–level officials came out from Washington. Some officials continued south to visit Antarctica. The usual routine was to arrange their visits with government ministers and to entertain them. In 1979, U.S. Secretary of the Interior Cecil Andrus came to New Zealand. As usual, he visited appropriate ministers. The Prime Minister and cabinet ministers hosted a lunch for him. Because his specialty was energy, he gave a speech on that topic for the entire embassy staff.

On November 28, 1979, I gave a dinner for Secretary Andrus at the embassy residence. There were twenty–three guests, among them David Lange, deputy leader of New Zealand's opposition party and later in 1983, Prime Minister. During dinner, my deputy, Terry Healey, was called to the telephone. On her return she murmured to me, "an Air New Zealand plane is missing."

One of the guests, a minister, received a similar call. If the plan had crashed, it would be catastrophic for New Zealand. Air New Zealand had enjoyed a splendid safety record. This would be the first crash to date of one of their planes. By the time most of the guests had left we had definite word that the plane had crashed into Mt. Erebus in Antarctica. Two hundred and twenty–seven tourists, most of them wearing light summer clothes and sandals, were scattered on the slopes. Ultimately, whatever they were wearing didn't matter, as all had died instantly.

"Captain Westbrook was right, Terry," I told my deputy, who stayed a few minutes after the guests left. "The Prime Minister wouldn't listen when I tried to warn him."

"You know you're scheduled to go to Antarctica to inspect the bases," Terry said. "Every ambassador visits the Antarctic for that purpose."

I knew such a trip might hold danger for me, but I had already enjoyed a full and interesting life; if something went wrong, I could not complain.

Captain Robert Scott, the famous British explorer, referred to the Antarctic as an awful place. I found it "awe–ful," in the biblical sense. Certainly it is the coldest, windiest, and least accessible of all the continents. Winds can exceed 200 miles an hour. A great deal of the world's weather originates in the Antarctic.

Dick Dols, the political officer, accompanied me on the trip to Antarctic. We went to Christchurch a day or two before our scheduled departure to try on the survival clothing we would be wearing for five days. I had sent my measurements for the garments: warm socks; lined rubber boots; wool shirts; thermal underwear; and red, lined parkas. Seeing me in survival clothing, Paree Ott, the American consular agent's wife who accompanied me to the base, said, "You look like a large red bear with white feet."

We left on December 9th, a Sunday morning, Captain Cranz introduced me to our companions on the trip. There were three scientists, a military man, and three crew members of the Hercules, a military transport plane. As I climbed into the aircraft, I saw a large yellow flatbed truck chained in the center. "Suppose it breaks loose?" I asked Dick.

"They secured it well, don't worry," he said.

The plane was stripped down. There were no windows. A few canvas bucket seats lined each side.

"I'm afraid this isn't luxury travel, Ambassador," the pilot said. "Behind that yellow plastic curtain, there's a chemical toilet. We call it the honey bucket."

After taking off, we sat quietly in the dark. I was nervous but also excited at the prospect of such an adventure. Five hours later, the Captain came back.

"Ambassador, would you like to join us on the flight deck? We can now see the continent of Antarctica."

"I'd love to."

For three hours I stood entranced, looking at the mysterious landscape.

"Did you know the landmass of Antarctica is as big as China?" asked the Captain.

I looked out at great rivers of ice flowing down the sides of the mountains. Like our Rockies, the mountains were rough and jagged, forming great promontories here and there. The highest peak was 16,000 feet. Because it was midsummer the sun rode high, gleaming on the ice below, casting shadows that ranged from turquoise to purple.

"When the sun is lower later in the year," the Captain said, "the ice shimmers in shades of rose and red. We're approaching the Ross Ice Shelf which was discovered by Sir James Clark Ross in 1841. Do you see down there—the ice floe and the icebergs breaking off from the shelf?"

"I see them. They're flat–topped."

"We're going to fly low. See out there, there's a group of Orcas, killer whales. You might like to see them closer."

The downward swoop was a little unnerving, but the close–up view of the whales drove everything else from my mind.

"Oh, look—they're rising out of the water and bowing to us!"

"Ahead of us," the Captain continued, "is Mt. Erebus, an active volcano. We'll fly around the crater."

He circled it three times but carefully avoided the crash site.

"We'll show you the crash site later," he said. "There are still bodies on the slope."

The United States and New Zealand had sent scientists and police officers to help with the clean up. I learned later that a family close to friends of mine at Hawkes Bay were victims: a grandmother had taken her entire family, children and grandchildren on the flight as her Christmas treat. They all died.

It was almost midnight when we landed, but it was full daylight. A dozen or so coffins stacked like logs in a woodpile rested near the spot where we landed. They were to go back to Christchurch with our plane.

A snow vehicle took us to McMurdo base. As we arrived, I saw a long, low, yellow building. "It looks like a cross between a trailer and a trolley," I told Dick.

Our escort showed us the windowless cubicles where we

were to sleep.

"There's a bath and a shower, but we hope you'll find sponge baths sufficient—we don't have much water. We're really situated in desert here and what water we have, we distill from the sea. Be sure to drink a lot if it because you must avoid dehydration."

We were roused for breakfast, available from six in the morning on. It was served cafeteria style, but nonetheless we had a menu. On it was a penguin wearing a chef's hat and his boast, "Every day a holiday—every meal a banquet." A sailor ahead of me in line helped himself to butter, hominy grits, three eggs, bacon, and a minute steak.

"That should hold you for a while," I said.

"Oh, I'm coming back for blueberry pancakes with syrup," he replied. He took his grub to a long table to join his mates.

After breakfast, we adjourned to the briefing room.

"Good morning, Ambassador. Today we'll show you photographs of the crash site and the recovery operations. Later we'll fly you to Mt. Erebus by helicopter," Captain Westbrook said.

In the black and white pictures, bodies were strewn over the snow like so many broken dolls.

"We don't know for certain the cause of the crash," the Captain said. "We do have some theories."

"Captain, obviously the airline broke its promise to fly higher than Mt. Erebus. They crashed halfway up the slope, didn't they?

"That's right, Ambassador. And faulty programming or instruments may have been part of the problem as well. I'm told no one on the flight deck had ever flown down here —if they had, they might have known they were off course. Probably there was a white–out. As you may know, in a white–out you have no reference. You could be flying upside down and not know it."

That afternoon a helicopter flew us to the crash site. All the bodies were gone, but fragments of the plane were scattered around the slope.

"They look like wood chips from this height," I said to the pilot. "Will you pick them up, too?"

"We're going to leave them there as a memorial."

After the trip to the crash site, a jeep took us on a tour of the base, which included the hut where Scott and his men lived while preparing for their overland trip to the Pole. Everything had been left exactly as it was sixty–two years earlier. It was as if they had just left for that race to the Pole in which they would be beaten by the Norwegian Roald Amundsen. Scott and his companions lost their lives in the attempt.

"Scott used Manchurian ponies to haul his sleds," our guide told me. "That was his biggest mistake—at least, it was the mistake that led to his death. Dogs are much more likely to survive this cruel climate than ponies."

All the New Zealand newspapers and reporters from quite a few from other countries flew down to cover the crash and cleanup. "The Kiwis [New Zealanders] were touching," one American investigator told me after the cleanup. "Their investigators and even their most hard–bitten reporters feel that it was their airline, their tragedy."

His comment didn't surprise me. I noticed how diligently they had all worked together for many days collecting the bodies. They were mourning. At a gathering held after the cleanup, one of the men told me, "No offense meant, Ambassador, but we'd like to call you Antarctic Annie. Hope you don't mind."

"I'll take it as a compliment," I said. I loved my new nickname.

The next morning we walked about two miles to Scott

Base, the New Zealand equivalent of McMurdo. Two of the men accompanying us carried a rough wooden cross they had made to place on the crash site. The parson read the burial service while thirty of us held hands in a circle. With tears in our eyes we said goodbye to the victims.

"Tomorrow, Ambassador," Captain Westbrook said after the service, "you and Mr. Dols will be flown to the South Pole. I've asked our most experienced pilot, 'Cadillac Jack,' to fly you. He's flown that trip two hundred and fifty–nine times."

After a four–hour flight, we reached South Pole Station, but Cadillac Jack had some trouble getting the skis on the plane down to land. When we landed, we learned the temperature was 32 degrees below zero. The warmest weather I had experienced on the trip was 36 degrees above zero at McMurdo, their summer temperature.

We walked to the circle of flags of the fourteen nations that had signed the Antarctic treaty in 1959. The flags were whipping in the wind. Next on the tour was the huge geodesic dome that covered four orange two–story buildings with scientific laboratories, a library, and sleeping quarters. One woman and nine men, our guide told us, would spend the winter at the pole this year.

"They'll stay all those cold dark months from February to November?" I asked.

"Yes, they keep very busy. Otherwise they'll go stir crazy."

Once inside the dome, we headed for the stairs. I felt a little claustrophobic and very out of breath.

"Take it easy, Ambassador, we're at twelve thousand feet. Most of that, of course, is ice on top of the landmass."

"Oh, I took a stress test in Washington and passed it —although the Navy doctor pushed me unmercifully."

We all climbed slowly, breathlessly, up six flights of

stairs to see the view.

"It looks as flat as Kansas—all that snow," I said. "I had expected to see the curve of the earth at the bottom of the world."

After lunch in the mess, I posted the Christmas cards that I had brought with me so that the cancellation mark would be the "South Pole." That afternoon Cadillac Jack flew us back to McMurdo.

The next day we visited the "dry valleys" by helicopter. There is no snow on the slopes there. The winds howl year–round, driving away the snow and carving the rocks into odd shapes. I saw shapes that resembled great chairs, birds, and figures that reminded me of Henry Moore's sculptures.

We lunched at Vanderlake station, a weather–monitoring outpost.

"Ambassador, we do have a ladies' room," said the pilot. You can be the first lady to visit it. It's there behind that yellow plastic curtain." While I was visiting the facility, a helicopter arrived. I felt I was only partly concealed.

On our next stop, the helicopter landed right on the ice. Near us a group of penguins were chattering below a glacier as high as a New York City skyscraper, and they seemed to be thoroughly enjoying themselves. I walked slowly toward them; they bowed. I mimicked their chatter; they bowed again. I bowed and, after some further interchange, waved goodbye. They bowed one last time—though I do not think I would have been surprised if they'd waved back.

As we hopped toward McMurdo, we passed over the penguins' rookery. We landed again on the ice and walked up to a mother seal and her baby. As I had learned from my penguin friends, you can get very close to the wildlife in Antarctica. They don't know that they have to be fearful.

Our five–day trip was drawing to a close. On the last day, Captain Westbrook conducted a farewell ceremony and

presented me with a plaque inscribed to "Antarctic Annie."
Cadillac Jack flew us back to Christchurch. From the flight
deck, I stared out at the mysterious continent that had
existed in the mind of man for so many centuries before it was
discovered. Fifteenth–century maps delineate it as "terra
Australias nondam cognita" or a southern land not yet known.

Captain Cook's ships that sailed within sight of
Antarctica were named for qualities that were needed for
exploration: *Endeavour* (1771) and the *Resolution* (1775); and
Shackleton's was named the *Endurance*. Four expeditions
went overland to the pole in the early 1900s, led by heroic
explorers who endured the suffering of those voyages with
resilience, cheerfulness, courage, and fellowship.

In the 1930s, Admiral Richard Byrd wintered alone
there in an advance base. In his book *Alone*, he described
the inner peace he felt as he contemplated a transcending
intelligence.

"The universe is not dead. Therefore, there is an Intelligence
there, and it is all pervading. At least one purpose, possibly
the major purpose, of that Intelligence is the achievement of
universal harmony. Striving in the right direction for Peace
(Harmony), therefore, as well as the achievement of it, is
the result of accord with that Intelligence. It is desirable
to effect that accord. The human race, then, is not alone in
the universe. Though I am cut off from human beings, I am
not alone. For untold ages man has felt an awareness of that
Intelligence. Belief in it is the one point where all religions
agree. It has been called by many names. Many call it God."

The year I visited was the twentieth anniversary
of the signing of the Antarctic Treaty. Renewed in 1990,
it guarantees that Antarctica shall be used exclusively for
peaceful purposes. Antarctica is the last frontier. There, if left
preserved, it will be possible to learn more about our earth
and in the process, ourselves.

Chapter Twelve

When the Maori Queen wrote me a letter of condolence for the three Americans killed in the Air New Zealand crash in early 1980, I thanked her and asked if I could visit her. She invited me to watch a race of the long canoes on the river near her residence on the North Island. Walter and Leo Clark, my North Country School friends, had just arrived for a visit and were included in the invitation.

There was a welcoming ceremony with warriors painted to look as if they were tattooed, chanting and shouting, shaking their spears, sticking out their tongues, and stamping their bare feet. That is the way Maori greet strangers, and on this occasion they were greeting not one but two ambassadors. The Australian Ambassador to New Zealand, who had arrived several months after I did, was also in attendance. We were all enchanted with the ceremony, the boat races, and the richness of the culture.

The following week I talked with the economic officer, Dick Imus.

"The best way to learn about a culture is to study the language," I said. "Even if I only learn a little, it will be fun. And appreciated, I should think."

Dick liked the idea so much he said he'd study with me. By the end of the week he'd found a deputy in the Maori Affairs Department, Charlie Mohi, to come to the Chancery twice a week to teach us.

I set about learning a speech: "*Ko Ana au,*" it began. "I am Anne." To the best of my knowledge, I am the only American Ambassador to have tried to learn Maori. I also learned that to be respected in Maori culture one had to come from a lake or a mountain.

"There's a lake in Princeton," I told Dick, "Carnegie Lake, four feet deep, nothing that would impress a Maori. But I have land in the Adirondacks, and there's a respectable mountain there – Whiteface, more than five thousand feet high. I think that's better, don't you?"

Dick and Charlie agreed.

"Now you are ready to make your speech," Charlie said after a few sessions. "I would like to invite you to my *marae*, my home village, for a weekend, and Mr. Imus as well, and of course, your families."

I told him that would be a "great honor and privilege," and that my visiting daughter and her family would love to come too. The date was set for a weekend.

"You just need to bring blankets or a sleeping bag. We will supply mattresses, pillows, and sheets. Everyone will sleep in the meeting house," Charlie said.

"I'm looking forward to the visit," my son–in–law, Allin Luther, said. "I'll read some books about the Maori. I want to make sure we don't violate their customs."

Allin bought four books and read them all, but he still had questions.

"You know, Ambassador," Charlie said on or about the tenth time I rang him, "you won't have to go down to the stream to brush your teeth. We do have a proper washhouse."

"I'm sorry to keep bothering you, but my son–in–law is a professor at the University of Michigan – and of German descent. He's determined to do the correct thing and not offend anyone."

Charlie chuckled. "Don't worry, they'll be very glad to see you."

"Where do we undress, as you said we'd all be together in the meetinghouse?"

"You hold up your blanket and undress as you would behind your towel at the beach."

I was never quite comfortable with that, so would turn in early.

We drove up from Wellington, the Luther family, the Imus family, and me. Charlie met us at the edge of the village as planned. He looked sheepish.

"Ambassador, our tribe always allows women to speak on our *marae*, the formal place for greeting, but at the moment we have a visiting tribe from the other side of the island that does not allow it. As they are our guests, we must defer to their customs. Will you appoint a talking chief?"

"Dick," I said, "here's the speech. I guess you'll have to give it for me." After all my studying, I was disappointed. I had not realized that Charlie's tribe was more liberated than most.

Outside the fence surrounding the *marae* we stood and listened while a woman gave the customary long musical calls to the ancestors announcing our arrival. The fence had wooden carvings of the ancestors' heads. The gates swung open and we walked forward a few paces into the space in front of the meetinghouse. There, warriors bearing spears, stuck their tongues out and shouted "*Hare ma–a–ai*" and danced the "welcoming" dance. Later I came to understand that the dance was a throwback to early times when tribes met strangers approaching their shores in a manner calculated to intimidate them.

After the dance and my speech – delivered by Dick – Charlie suggested we have tea.

"Then," he said, "we will go into Hastings so that you may see our visitors perform."

"Perform what?" I asked him.

"They will dance and sing. They are raising money to go to America."

The auditorium in Hastings was large and packed with people. The "visitors" were students from Waikato University – lissome young women in grass skirts and handsome bronzed young men decorated with paint in patterns similar to the ancient Maori tattoos. They sang and danced with grace and precision.

"It's very different, isn't it, from the performances put on for tourists?" Charlie said.

Allin, who had not really wanted to come because he was afraid we might offend someone, was now taping the performance with a small recorder he'd brought along.

Back at the *marae*, there was more tea and snacks and beer.

"I'm going to retire to my mattress," I said. I was tired and wanted to undress in private.

Allin and Marjory stayed up late talking to the young performers. It was an active night. According to the students, "the professor" who accompanied them enjoyed the beer and had to be walked out, over the mattresses, from time to time to relieve himself. We were so close together that when one person turned, everyone had to turn.

"I can't find my shoes," I told one of the students the next morning. "I do have another pair, but could you look for them?"

Several students looked, but they said they could not find the shoes.

That morning we had a huge breakfast, which included lamb stew. Charlie said, "There'll be a church service in a few minutes, but you don't have to attend."

Of course, we went. The service was held in the front of the meetinghouse. Charlie was an elder of the Mormon congregation, and the hymns – most of them familiar – were sung in Maori. There were a number of Mormon congregations within the Maori population.

"*Tapu, tapu, tapu*" was "Holy, holy, holy."

Charlie spoke after the hymns and prayers in English.

"I am going to tell you the story of this *marae*," he began. "Up there at the peak of the roof of our meetinghouse is a carving. It represents my grandmother, the daughter of the paramount chief of the Eastern Tribe.   "After the Maori chiefs asked Queen Victoria if New Zealand could join the British Empire in 1840, many of our tribes felt we should employ a British agent to help us handle our affairs. This tribe employed a Scotsman. His name was Cooper and he was given the paramount chief's daughter in marriage. They also gave him considerable land and built this house for them."

"She soon bore him a son, who was my father. A year or two later, Mr. Cooper went home to Scotland for a year's leave. He returned bringing with him a Scottish bride." Charlie paused for a moment. "He had not taken the Maori marriage seriously. The elders felt pretty nasty about that. They moved the meeting house here, my grandmother lived here alone with her baby...."

Later, when I told this story to my *pakeha* (the Maori word for non–Maori) friends, they said, "How awful; Cooper is written up in history books as a settler who became very rich."

On the way home from Charlie's *marae*, Allin and Marjory told me about their conversations with the students.

"They're discriminated against," Marjory said. "They have the lowest paid jobs, the most limited opportunities."

"But New Zealand treats their minorities – Maori and Pacific Islanders – far better than we've treated our Native Americans. And infinitely better than the Australians treat the Aborigines," I said.

"All the same," Allin said, "there's deep resentment."

Although I hadn't talked to them myself, I sensed that he was right. Allin had a way of drawing out young people and, as an expert on Iran, he had accumulated a great deal of experience in speaking to people from various cultures.

A week later I had lunch in Auckland with a visiting *New York Times* reporter who'd promised to investigate the situation and let me know what he found out.

"I've spent two days visiting Pacific Islanders and Maori," he told me later. "I had coffee this morning with a Maori family. The father was out of work, the mother was out of work, and there was an eighteen–year–old daughter who worked briefly but then lost her job. There were several younger children…"

"Tell me more," I said.

"I grew up in a middle–class family in Queens. I asked the Maori family what they paid in rent, how much they spent on groceries and other expenses such as their car. Then I asked what the government gave them, the dole. What they had to live on would be considered a middle–class income in Queens."

"That's reassuring."

"Yes, Ambassador. I don't think there's going to be ethnic trouble here in New Zealand."

"Hopefully, you're right," I said. "But, you know, money isn't the only issue. They want recognition and status."

When the Te Maori exhibition came to the Metropolitan Museum in New York in 1984, after my return from New Zealand, Charlie was one of the elders who accompanied the show. Carol O'Biso, the registrar of the show for the American Federation of the Arts, described the six elders in the opening of her book *First Light*:

"At first light I heard it. A pale dusting of morning crept between buildings in the east and with it came the greeting call, '*Haere ma–a–ii.*' It rose above the city, above the chortling of the early buses making their way down Fifth Avenue, off key, warbling a little, and then it reached a crescendo. The sound diminished softly into the hugeness of the city.

The warriors in loincloths and bare feet moved slowly down the Avenue from 84th Street. In the lead was a tall, striking man who had golden–brown skin and a long mane of snowy white hair. The procession of the Maori moved slowly, all of them chanting in unison and praying, and the warriors danced ahead, thrusting with their spears, eyes darting, fending off the spirits, clearing the way for the elders of their land. They reached the foot of the steps...."

Clearly the Maori dancers were as riveting to New Yorkers as they had been to me.

At the evening reception after the procession, Charlie confided, "Do you know what happened to the shoes you could not find when you visited us in Hastings?"

"No, I wondered."

"They are in a glass case at Waikato University. The students must have taken them as a momento."

"Oh dear – I wish my feet were as small as Cinderella's!"

The Te Maori show generated tremendous interest in the Maori culture here in the United States. Featuring traditional Maori artwork, the exhibition was first shown in New York, and then travelled around the country. For perhaps the first time in this country Americans learned that the Maori make up 10 to 11 percent of the population of New Zealand. Some of New Zealand's most talented artists have Maori blood, including the famous lyric soprano Kiri Te Kanawa and her mentor, John Matheson, conductor of Sadler's Wells orchestra and of Covenant Garden in England. I am grateful to Charlie Mohi and other Maori friends who gave me the opportunity to understand New Zealand's rich cultural mix and the role New Zealand plays interpreting Polynesian culture to the world.

*   *   *   *   *

The hostage–taking in Iran hung like a dark cloud over most of the time I was in New Zealand. I had some insight into the situation through my son–in–law Allin Luther, who was head of the American–Iranian Foundation. Allin had visited Tehran, as he did every year, two or three months before the hostage taking at the embassy. His many Iranian friends all warned him that if the Shah were allowed to enter the United States there would be trouble. Almost certainly the embassy would be attacked, and hostages would probably be taken.

For years, the U.S. Embassy in Tehran staff would not give Allin's fears any credence – he was just a professor. At the American Embassy in Teheran, with a staff of nearly eight hundred, only three spoke Farsi, the language of the country. But by 1979 what was left of the staff in Tehran hung on to Allin's words. They did not dare leave their compound. Allin reported to them the information circulating in Tehran.

When Allin returned, he went to Washington and walked the corridors of the State Department trying to get someone to listen. He talked to the desk officers who agreed with his analysis, but above that level no one would talk to him. I would have called the White House in a minute on his behalf, but I was in New Zealand at the time and I did not know.

The hostages were taken, as Allin predicted. Night after night on the news, Walter Cronkite intoned the number of days they were held prisoners. In my diary of January 1981, after the election, I wrote: "The world is now at a standstill until Reagan takes over, but it's poised, taking a deep breath, waiting to see what happens."

Warren "Chris" Christopher, deputy secretary of state, had been negotiating in Algeria; the rest of us were all praying that the release would take place before the inauguration. The State Department instructed me to thank the New Zealand government for helping some U.S. personnel escape.

As it turned out, the ayatollah would not reward Carter. He waited until 6:05 a.m. on January 20th, Inauguration Day, to announce that the hostages were on a plane and out of the Iranian air space. Their release at that particular moment had quite a few people, including me, wondering if there was collusion between President–elect Reagan and the Ayatollah.

*   *   *   *   *

By late February 1981, with a new President in the White House, I realized it was time to pay my official farewell calls to the mayors and other public dignitaries around the country. Shortly after Christmas I had visited Toss Woollaston, one of New Zealand's best known painters, and his wife, Edith, on a tour of the South Island with its gigantic Atlas Cedars and Dawn Cypress trees and flourishing rose gardens.

On the way to Dunedin, we stopped at a famous beach to see the Moaroki boulders, great spherical stones 60 million years old. They are about six feet across and smooth; some in shallow water, some on the beach, some emerging from the face of the cliff.

We arrived in Dunedin and had a tour of the town, guided by a professor from the university. Dunedin is a quintessential university town, with buildings made of granite and exuding a sense of learning and permanence.

Most of my day was taken up with appointments. I met with the local member of parliament, the mayor, and went to the newspaper for an interview. My aunt Marise, who accompanied me, said, "If this is the kind of schedule you have everywhere, you really earn your pay."

"Thank you, Marise, it is what I am here for. Tomorrow

I'll have a similar schedule in Invercargill. Then we'll fly
to Stewart Island for the weekend. We can't call on anyone
Saturday or Sunday."

Marise wrote in her letter describing the trip, "Stewart
Island is very large and wild, and has a total population of
600 people, nine–tenths of them are fishermen. The birds are
wonderful. The New Zealand wood pigeon is enormous, has a
white waistcoat, an iridescent green head and beak, and red
eyes. Another big bird is a Weka, which is the size of a big
chicken with golden brown feathers, red legs, and red beaks.
They are tame; one walked into our bedroom in our motel.
We went out in a fishing boat and saw hundreds of blue
penguins and thousands of Mutton birds, which are really
big black shearwaters. We fished on lines with two hooks for
blue cod, hauling up two at a time. As we returned we saw
a fur seal. He had just caught an octopus and was trying to
subdue it. He'd come to the surface and, wham, went the seal:
He struck the octopus – slap, slam – on top of the water. He
must have done it at least 15 times while we watched, not ten
feet away. We took a walk through the bush. We saw many
different varieties of ferns and mosses, and tiny wild orchids.
We were serenaded by Bell birds, whose delicious song put
nightingales to shame."

My last months were marked by official visits and plans
for departure. I found it very hard to say goodbye to good
friends. Malcolm and Paree Ott, who adopted me as a member
of their family from the beginning of my tenure, and who
still live in Christchurch. The walls of the Ott's big Victorian
house are hung with Paree's abstract paintings and a portrait
of the artist by Olivia Spencer Bower, herself a well–known
artist. Malcolm Ott was the consular agent for the United
States in Christchurch, although he is a New Zealand citizen.

Then there was Toss and Edith Woollaston. Edith was
lovely, tolerant, generous, and other–worldly; Toss was New

Zealand's leading artist, the only painter ever knighted by the
Queen of England. He actually considered declining the honor
of being knighted until he learned that if he did, it would
very likely be offered to an artist for whom he had no respect.

When I went for my first visit to the Woollastons in
October, Toss met me at the corner in front of the post office
in Motueka. My diary records that I found him there as "eager
as a boy."

"Charlie, it's been a good two years," I said to my
deputy a few days before I left. "You have been a wonderful
help to me."

"You know how much I've enjoyed working with you,
Ambassador. You know the inspector gave us high marks —
unusually high marks."

"You should take credit for that."

"It's to your credit, especially. And Secretary Holbrooke
gave you a wonderful letter of commendation.

"It was nice of him, and I appreciate it. I wonder,
Charlie, how life will develop here in the next few years. New
Zealand was one of the first socialist countries; I wonder how
they will maintain their generous health care system that
covers everyone from cradle to grave. Even though there's
no capital gains tax, income taxes are enormous. Right now
hardly anyone has a net income of over twenty thousand
dollars."

"I wonder, too. Their debt is so high. I do think
Labor will be elected—by 1984, if not this year. There's an
interesting fellow, Roger Douglas, who would like to be finance
minister. I've read what he proposes; vast changes including
privatization of state-owned enterprises. But he would keep
many of the early programs – health care, for example. The
other change may be in the security arrangement. I worry
about that. Sooner or later the peace activists may force the
Labor Party's hand on anti-nuclear policy. That will threaten

the ANZUS Alliance."

"I'm glad I won't be Ambassador if that happens. I shall miss 'the land of the Long White Cloud.' It is the most beautiful country on earth, and I've been in more than eighty countries. I love the southern Alps. Mt. Cook is over 12,000 feet. And so many mountains are covered with eternal snow. And those breathtaking long arms of the sea reaching into Fjorland, where waterfalls leap off the cliffs. The Bay of Islands above Auckland beats Maine and Puget Sound for bays dotted with pine–clad islands—and for fishing, the trout and salmon leap out onto fishermen's lines!"

"You have been nearly everywhere in New Zealand; I don't think any ambassador ever got about as much."

After I left in the early 1980s, relations between New Zealand and America became strained when the new Labor Prime Minister refused to allow a United States naval ship to enter a New Zealand port without declaring if they carried nuclear weapons. To help ease the tension, I founded the United States/New Zealand Council hoping to rebuild the ANZUS Alliance threatened by this action. Over the years relations have improved, in part because of the Council. As part of the United Nations deployment, New Zealand and Australia had earlier fought alongside the United States in the Korean War. Later, New Zealand sent transport aircraft, maritime patrol aircraft, and frigates to the Iraq war, as well as a very small number of soldiers, SAS soldiers, medical and peace–keeping forces to Afghanistan—and despite Prime Minister Helen Clark being openly critical of American justifications for the war, New Zealand did send engineers and troops to Iraq.

But there were other legacies from my time in New Zealand, some I was about to discover.

Chapter Thirteen

Early one morning only months before leaving New Zealand, Jim Barr, director of Dowse Gallery in Lower Hutt, invited me to the opening of an exhibition of two of the country's most prominent artists, Colin McCahon and Toss Woollaston. I had bought a drawing by Woollaston recently, *Bayly's Hill* and looked forward to our meeting.

The opening was on a Saturday, my driver's day off. So I made the trip from the residence to the gallery on my bicycle. Jim Barr met me near the entrance, amused by my means of transportation. When he introduced me to Toss, he characterized me as "the ambassador from the United States who rode over here on her bike." It occurred to me, years later, that I might have remained just acquaintances with Toss and his wife Edith had I swept up in the big black car, flags flying. Instead, they became good friends.

Toss was only slightly taller than I; his sandy hair was always tousled, and his blue eyes sparkled with humor. Part of his attraction lay in his energy; he radiated vigor, vitality, and wit. Toss took the role of guide. First, he led me into a large room where several of Colin McCahon's big black canvases were hung. Biblical phrases in white lettering were scattered over them.

"They're interesting," I said after looking at them for a while, "but I find them depressing. I don't like black."

"But you should," said Toss, who then described how Renoir reacted when some of his students told him they'd thrown their tubes of black paint into the Seine. Renoir said, "But why did you do that? Black is a beautiful color!"

195

Colin McCahon, Toss explained, was an excellent painter who felt that "art should send a message; it should be used as propaganda. "He has painted a canvas titled *Landscape with too few Lovers,* which is largely the way he felt about New Zealand. I feel differently."

We walked into the next gallery to look at Toss's paintings. I stood entranced. Great vigorous strokes of paint swept across the canvas. There was the deep blue of the sea, above it a small patch of green–blue sky. In between were mountains, golden shading to rose. The forests on the hills were a dark shade of green, almost black. This was the landscape I was learning to love as Joe, my driver, drove me the length and breadth of New Zealand in the big, black car on our official rounds.

"Your landscape is full of light!"

"I wanted to paint the color of sunlight, but only after it had been absorbed by the earth."

When Toss asked me if I painted, I admitted to being a Sunday painter.

"Perhaps you'd like to come out with me sometime. I'm painting here now—working on views of the Wellington Harbor, so I come often to Wellington. I'll be here next week, in fact."

"Do come, stay at the residence, and bring Lady Woollaston with you."

And so it began. They arrived late the following week. We were all invited to a party at the house of the financier Robert Jones, whose portrait Toss had painted. Most of the weekend was quiet, and I was delighted to spend some time talking to Edith while Toss went out to paint. Edith was a rare and wonderful woman. We became friends at once.

Edith was in her mid–seventies, five years older than Toss, and was quite beautiful. Her figure was graceful, her fair Scottish skin only faintly wrinkled. Her fine bone structure gave her face a beautiful shape. Her lovely spirit shone through her large, luminous, gray eyes. I loved the faint Scottish intonation of her voice that always reminded me of my dear Grandpa Clark.

I told her about Grandpa, my favorite relative. Edith told me about her father, a Scotsman from Aberdeen, who after he came to New Zealand, was appointed the city engineer in Dunedin.

"Tell me about your family," she said. "What was your mother like?"

"Unhappy," I said. "Almost always. She agonized over my father's interest in other women. But I'm not sure that she wouldn't have been unhappy anyway. The one period during which I think she enjoyed her life was during the war, when she worked for the Red Cross."

As I talked, the old pain of my childhood washed over me: anger at my father for hurting my mother so often and so deeply; anger toward my mother for her inability to cope with his cruelty; and finally, the old familiar anger at myself.

Edith must have sensed my feelings. "It is hard to find the courage to fight when you are crushed. I've observed that mothers and daughters often repeat this pattern. Was that true of you?"

"Yes, I'm afraid it was. Jackson Martindell was an attractive man. He liked women, especially young ones. Like my father, he had a roving eye. There was a time, copying my mother, when I made myself miserable about Jackson's affairs. I realize now it was a waste of time."

"I never felt that way," Edith said. "I always felt that I could never be that possessive, even if Toss was interested in someone else. We would talk it over. I know that his love for me will always be there. I'll always come first."

"I'm sure that's true. It's wonderfully generous of you," I said.

Toss told me how much love meant to Edith. His stories about his childhood clearly indicated that sex itself was very important to him, as well as love.

I thought again, as I had many times, how different my parents' marriage and my childhood might have been if Mummy had been less possessive or if she had been able to fight back. If only she had been able to understand that she was important to Father; that he really loved her best. He was devastated when she wouldn't take him back after the war. She asked for a divorce.

Edith and Toss gathered their things.

"Promise to visit us soon. Toss will be back to paint, but I'll look forward to seeing you in Motueka," said Edith.

Toss came again to visit and I went out to paint with him. We talked at length, about his childhood and mine—so different, of course. We talked about art, about music, about books—everything but politics. Toss was not interested in politics, although his youngest son had been elected to Parliament. All the while he would talk about love, about how he could make me happy, about what we could do together. It was a courtship and very exciting. We did not kiss; I seldom remember holding hands. Toss, however, was a poet as well as a painter, and he wooed me with words. It was very effective. I was comfortable knowing that I wasn't hurting Edith—that she and Toss had an understanding.

Toss came back the following week. We drove up to KoroKoro where there was a view over the Wellington Harbor, past Soames Island to the headlands and the sea. So, our friendship, in a way, began inside one of his great landscapes.

Toss sat on his camp stool, a basket filled with pads, pens, and watercolor paints at his feet. He looked at the scene before him; I sat quietly by.

"Sometimes," he said after a while, "I sit and look for as long as two hours, while I realize the scene."

He needed less time that particular day as he was familiar with the view. Watching him, I thought I could almost see the process: his eye conveyed the landscape to his mind, rejecting some components and accepting others.

"I use only a few colors," he said. "Yellow ocher, light red, permanent blue, viridian, and titanium white."

He told me that "as a sort of shorthand" he often made small rectangles in the corner of the canvas to reduce the composition to a few main shapes. "One way to define art is as a selection of things from the scene."

He had studied Ostwald's theories about color—which combinations resulted in harmonious contrasts—then settled me down with my oil paints, and he set to work. After looking closely at the landscape, sorting out the elements, considering others, he took pen in hand. His pen flew here and there on the sketch pad, constructing the drawing in a few swift stokes.

He talked as he sketched. "Cézanne said to paint is to contrast."

After the drawing was finished, he began a watercolor on a separate sheet of paper. Once he started painting, his hand darted like a bird over the paper, bringing clear, vivid colors to life. When Toss finished and put away his paints, he turned to me.

"Tell me about your life. Is there someone special for you here or at home?"

"My husband and I have been separated for eleven years."

"I had a close friend for ten years," said Toss, "We parted recently because she became jealous of Edith. I couldn't put up with that."

"Edith told me that whatever might happen, she knows she will always come first."

"Indeed she does come first, she always will. Our love for each other is strong."

We got into the car in silence. I was in a tumult of emotion. I had never been as attracted to a man as I was to Toss, and I felt that he was attracted to me.

I discovered from talking to friends that the so–called "open marriage" had become popular in New Zealand in certain circles. To some people, the relationship Jackson and I had may have been viewed as an "open marriage," but it was only "open" as far as Jackson was concerned. Yet, it was not the norm with most of the people I knew.

Toss apparently discussed his love affairs in a very candid manner with Edith. He felt it important to be honest and open. I could admire that attitude. The result of that honesty, that I would be a "third wheel" in their marriage should I enter into a relationship with Toss, made me very uncomfortable. I was particularly concerned because I admired Edith and did not in any way want to be the cause of any unhappiness to her.

On the way back to the residence, Toss told me about his childhood on a remote farm in Taranaki. He was the eldest of five boys. His autobiography *Sage Tea* opens with, "My mother wished I had been a daughter;" she longed for a female companion. She was creative. Her passion was music, especially Bach. Toss told me that from the age of five, he knew he wanted to be an artist. I doubted that statement until I read any early autobiographical sketch that he had written. At school he excelled in drawing and composition.

He hated farm work and was determined to get away from the farm as soon as possible. In his autobiography, Toss recounted his escape from the religious oppression of his parents. Their method of bringing up boys to be "good" was to terrify them with fear of a vengeful God who would send them to eternal damnation if, for example, they used the Lord's name in vain. Sexual repression went along with it. His young brothers were rougher and tougher, and seemed to thrive on daily discipline, but Toss wrestled with his own awakening sexuality and would lie awake at night suffering terrible fears of damnation. Art was a path to freedom, one way of escaping the constraints of his childhood.

The next time Toss returned to Wellington, I went out to paint with him again. The watercolors he worked on that day were the basis for one of his great Wellington paintings. In an early watercolor study I appeared in my pink raincoat, although in the final painting I'm just a figure. Toss, as he worked, explained what he was doing. He quoted the artist Hans Hoffman: "Feelings are a gift of God, but theory is a help to the feelings when they are not in their best condition." Toss was a man full of feeling; feeling transformed and permeated his painting. His approach to painting, indeed to life, was a revelation to me. I had been taught to repress emotion and that appearances mattered more than anything. Toss was absolutely honest, in painting and his relations with Edith and his friends. His honesty was infectious, and I found myself confronting my own feelings with the same degree of candor. By the time I was invited to spend a weekend with Toss and Edith, I knew I was falling in love with him. In a few months I would be going back to America; nine thousand miles would separate us. I might never see him again.

After arriving in Motueka, Toss and I drove to a painting site that had a marvelous view of Tasman Bay. It was late afternoon, the sun's rays were sending horizontal shafts through the branches of the trees. Below were ferns. We lay among them; their scent enveloped us. It was there that the love affair began with the man who became the love of my life.

It was soon that I had to leave, sadly soon, as Toss wrote in a letter. I wondered if I should rent a house near his. That thought did not last long. Toss was attractive to many women; there would have been too much competition, too many eyes watching. I had to wait.

At the house in Motueka, the weather was sunny and warm. Edith and I often sat on the veranda overlooking the garden and watched Toss bend lovingly over the lettuce he had planted.

"With Toss," Edith said, "gardening is a passion. Painting is simply his vocation." Edith sat stroking her beloved white cat, Yin. She wore a simple cotton dress, her gray pigtail down her back. Grapevines climbed the posts of the veranda that encircled the house.

"You built this house, didn't you?" I asked.

"Yes, we had a Chinese architect who admired Frank Lloyd Wright. He liked the simplicity of unpainted concrete blocks. Originally, there was an old house on the property. We lived in it until this house was finished. Toss did all the planning with the architect. He talked to me about it often." Edith said.

"Did Toss plan the garden, too?"

"We discussed it together. I had been a professional gardener at the Botanical Gardens in Dunedin."

"I love the way the flowers and vegetables flourish side by side in your garden—potatoes, tomatoes, herbs near the roses, sweet peas, poppies, and lilies. Every inch seems to be planted." I paused. "Toss's life is really one long love affair with New Zealand, isn't it?" I said.

My last few weeks in New Zealand were a whirlwind. Here I was falling in love with a man who loved his wife and his country. I was hosting Speaker Tip O'Neill and other American dignitaries. And I was consumed with the routine of departing ambassadors, which is to call on all the government ministers. Surprisingly, the Prime Minister thanked me for my tenure.

Upon my arrival back to Princeton, I found a letter from Toss waiting for me:

14 May 1981

Dear Anne,

Ten days since you left. If this beats you home,
"Welcome home! If not, it shouldn't be that long
after. I hope you had a good rest on the way and will
be fit for whatever you have to do at home before you
can slip away and court boredom. Neil McGrath (of
Lower Hutt) was here yesterday and remarked that
the sketch–like painting of the view from KoroKoro is
more dramatic than his (Drunk with newness, not yet
sobered down by hard work?). I haven't yet started on
the finished version with you in it.

Edith sends her love with mine.

Toss

* * * * *

Reentry was not easy. I missed my deputy, Charlie
Salmon, and Joe, my driver. I was lonely for my New Zealand
friends, particularly Toss and Edith. My own country seemed
noisy and traffic–filled. The air was heavy with pollution,
and the water tasted terrible. Of course I was happy to be
surrounded once again by family and good friends, and I even
told a few of them about Toss and Edith.

Letters flew back and forth; their frequency made me realize that Toss would not disappear from my life. Although I made two trips to New Zealand, seeing Toss and Edith briefly each time, Toss and I were not able to arrange to be together alone.

In 1986, Toss stopped to see me after a trip to Spain. He loved Spain and admired the great Spanish painters, particularly Velasquez and Goya. He painted his own version of Velasquez's *Las Meninas*.

At that time I had a one room apartment in New York. There we were able to be together all night, every night. The pent–up desire and love from five years earlier flowered and grew. We drew closer together in mutual ecstasy. Toss was able to make love continually, it seemed, for hours. I loved his strong, muscular body. I never tired of it, every inch always excited me. I had never experienced such intensive lovemaking. Toss said, "You are the only woman I have ever known that liked sex as much as I do." In many respects, it was Toss who allowed me to realize that truth.

It was hard for me to imagine what the other women were like, how could they not respond? Edith, of course, was in a different category. For Toss she was on a pedestal, I was not. Toss was eager, passionate yet tender, imaginative, and indefatigable. He was in love with me and I with him.

We drove to Trenton so I could show him where I used to sit as a senator and walked around Princeton University's campus. We sat for some time in the chapel. The beautiful stained–glass windows cast rainbows on the floor as the sun shone through them. Toss said that "in a few more centuries" they might be like the ones at the Cathedral in Chartres, France.

After Toss returned to New Zealand, there was a long silence. Finally, late in September, a sad letter came. Toss said Edith had had a stroke in August, she was in the Nelson

Hospital for a while, then in the annex. She could walk with support but was mostly in a wheelchair. Toss visited her every day. He bought some land in Nelson, planning to build a house when she was released from the hospital. If necessary, he planned to give up painting to look after her.

One day, he wrote, he visited her around noon. She told him to go out and paint. Two hours later he returned. "She was gone." She'd had another, this time fatal, stroke. She was 82.

At first, Toss was devastated. My letters of sympathy were so inadequate. When Toss began to heal, he wrote: "If I can survive Edith's death, I can survive anything."

*   *   *   *   *

Toss wrote occasionally after Edith's death, seeming depressed and confused. Around Christmas of 1988 he wrote that he was coming to the States to visit his friend Tim Francis, who was the Ambassador to the United States from New Zealand. He planned to visit him in Washington in January. He asked if he could visit me also.

I had been working with Tim to improve relations between our two countries through the United States/New Zealand Council. I wrote Toss that I would be delighted to see him, but I would be very busy with the Council. He complained about that.

Toss came to Princeton. When we talked about his travel plans, I suggested that he visit Santa Fe before returning home. "Dozens of artists have loved those landscapes and the light in the Southwest," I told him. "I'll go with you. I was there last summer and loved it."

A short time later we arrived in Albuquerque. As

we drove across the desert, Toss became more and more excited. "This is Zane Grey country," he exclaimed joyously. As a boy he had devoured Zane Grey's books with their vivid descriptions of landscape. (Gray had first visited New Zealand in 1926, at the age of 54, to indulge his interest in deep–sea fishing.) On the edge of town we found our rented condominium, an adobe abode, fake adobe at that.
We explored the town. "The street signs are all in Spanish," Toss said, "but I don't hear anyone speaking Spanish."

We explored the countryside, but mostly explored each other. Friendship had deepened into love. Toss wrote in his diary: "It is seven thousand feet high here. It started snowing at midday on Monday, and by Tuesday morning there were four inches of new dry snow and all the trees were hung with it like trees in a Christmas card. The evergreens had fragile knife–like snow, blades up, balanced on all their branches, proving there had been no wind while the snow was falling…"

We went inside to our small living room and had a cup of tea in front of the mesquite fire. After a moment or two of companionable silence, Toss suggested that we might get married. He said his mother had always recommended that all married couples spend six months apart. By that time I was deeply in love with him—after having assumed for many years that I could never, ever really fall in love. When I told him I'd consider it—seriously—he understood that my answer was yes. But even then, in the first rush of joy and excitement, I saw hazards. Could I move to New Zealand and leave my family? It didn't seem possible. Could I encourage him to live in the U.S. and leave not only his family but also the roots that nourished his art? Would six months together out of a year work?

We continued this discussion over the remainder of this trip and then by letter—Toss excited about the prospect of marriage, and I was weighing all the potential pitfalls. My children were pleased about this new love in my life, but the priest at Trinity Church and my lawyer expressed serious reservations about managing a marriage on two continents.

I wrote to Toss that perhaps marriage was not the best answer. He wrote back:

Dear Anne,

Now that marriage is off, it is a relief in a way. That you don't have to be made "an honest woman" of is quite in keeping with modern manners and customs, and I am happy with it. My only regret is that I told my family and one or two special friends. Two of my sons accepted the announcement with reserve ("if that's what you want, Dad") but Philip and Chan, and my daughter Anna were thrilled. I don't know what to say to them now. It is pride, perhaps, I feel I've been silly. I am, of course, wondering what made you change your mind—and guessing I know.

When I suggested marriage, it was precisely because you wanted to be made an honest woman of! Are you likely to change any more?

Lots of love,

Toss

That letter distressed me. I really had not changed my mind; he had jumped to that conclusion. Living with a man without the church's blessing was difficult for me. Yet the practicalities of marriage were difficult. Toss needed New Zealand to inspire his art, and I needed my family to nourish my life. Clearly we would have to arrange periods of time when we could be together and periods of time when we would live apart. It would take some getting used to. Toss's authenticity helped me jump some of the hurdles of "appearance" and "convention," and finally I embraced our arrangement.

Toss returned to the United States in June. We rented a house in Pojaque, near Santa Fe, for a month. Eugenia, the part–time housekeeper, and Bob, and Chris, who looked after the garden, came with the house. They were highly knowledgeable about Native American culture. Bob, who lived on a reservation, was especially helpful. Toss sketched one of Bob's friends, a well–known Indian potter, then completed a watercolor of his subject. The potter looked from the painting to Toss, then back to the painting.

"Is that me?" he asked.

Also sharing the house were an old neurotic dog and two sweet black puppies who one day walked dusty–footed all over a canvas Toss had prepared with gesso and laid flat on the brick patio to dry.

"Oh, no," I exclaimed when I saw what happened, "you'll have to get a new canvas and start over."

"Not at all," he said. "The paw prints will give the canvas a nice texture!"

When it was dry, he knelt on the floor with his drawings and watercolors of the view from the Opera House beside him and painted, in oils, what was to become the Santa Fe painting in his retrospective show. That show, held in 1992 in New Zealand, provided an occasion for art critics to look at his career to date and say—not for the first time —that not only was he the greatest Australasian painter, but that he could have been a painter of renown in any country at any period.

Toss often sketched the wriggly puppies, convinced that it loosened up his drawing and helped his painting. Every time a plane flew over, he watched its progress—a habit that inspired *The Big Sky*, a painting of Tasman Bay as viewed from a prone position looking up at an airplane. I have this painting hanging in my living room.

We stayed in Santa Fe for a month, then returned to Princeton so Toss could meet my friends. They all loved him. We visited the Adirondacks. Toss described the mountains as the "leaping Adirondacks" and confessed he couldn't quite get the rhythm of them.

When Toss went back to New Zealand I missed him, but his letters were loving and filled with excitement about our relationship. I felt fulfilled and complete for the first time in my life. He was everything that a man should be to a woman—kind, loving, interesting. I kept saying to myself, "How can I be so lucky?"

In October I went out to New Zealand to join him. We were sitting at the breakfast table in his house one morning with the sunlight pouring in the big window. Toss raised his eyebrows, crinkled his brow, and said:

"I think Edith would be very happy about us."

I looked past him to the veranda, festooned with vines. I could almost see her there, smiling at us.

Chapter Fourteen

All seven hundred and fifty of the Smith Class of 2002 stood up in the bright May sunshine, shouting, stomping, cheering and waving. The President of the college was about to hand me, Anne Clark Martindell, an honorary degree in Law, Honoris Causa. What would my father have thought now? Last year, my brother Bill had asked me, "Do you think he's listening?" I know that my mother would have been proud—just as she was when I was sworn in as Senator. All thirty–five of my children, grandchildren, nieces, nephews, and a few close friends were cheering along with the crowd. I would receive dozens of letters of congratulations, among them one from Senator Ted Kennedy, who observed that I had surpassed even Kennedy record for family attendance at such an event.

I welcomed the presence of my children on the occasion of my graduation from Smith, for our bonds had been strengthened over the years, and they had grown into adults I respected as well as loved. Marjory continues to live in Ann Arbor, where she has been active in her church and served as the organizer of the Hunger Coalition for many years; George, an investment banker, would probably most like to model himself on the explorer John Ledyard, our distant relative, who was the first American to see the coast of Washington and Oregon, as well as New Zealand, Australia, Tahiti and Hawaii; David has been an executive in the publishing business for many years; Roger is a lawyer and has been a member of the Borough Council of Princeton for sixteen years. His proficiency in Spanish has helped him work closely with the Hispanic community on issues of equality and fair employment practices. I've tried to emphasize to them that being of service to one's community is more important than chasing the dollar, and their lives bear witness to that truth.

The years of hard work, of dozens of books read and absorbed were behind me, somewhat to my regret. Going back to Smith had been a wonderful experience, I loved every minute of it. I loved walking around the campus designed by Frederick Law Olmstead, who designed Central Park where I played as a young child. I loved poking around the Lyman greenhouse with its peaked glass roof. I loved searching in the stacks for the right book for a paper, loved the rare book room where I hardly dared to speak above a whisper. I loved the studio art course up the hill where I learned enough about photography while taking pictures around Northampton to know that I had a good "eye," a skill I hope to continue using. "Learning more" is still my objective. I hope that much more lies ahead, even though so much lies behind.

And above all I hope to encourage other women to plunge into life—long learning, to open up to new experience. Some years ago I heard a rich women say, "When I wake up in the morning, I hate it. It is just another day of wondering how I can fill the hours." I am told that there are over 32 million American women over sixty, some widowed, and some divorced, and some retired. Many feel that life for them is virtually over; a little golf or bridge, perhaps, or a good book and television. They wait for calls from children. If only I could encourage them to follow the interests and passions they put aside. At fifty nine, I was elected to the State Senate; a sixty—three I was appointed Director of the Office of Foreign Disaster Assistance; at sixty—five I became Ambassador to New Zealand; at sixty—six I fell truly in love for the first time. At seventy—four, after his wife died, Toss proposed—so I spent the last years of his life with him.

There was an element of luck, which played a part. But if one stays active and involved, there is often a point at which one can seize opportunities that would not come to anyone sitting passively at a bridge table or in front of a television set. A friend told me that his mother–in–law, age sixty–seven, had come for a visit. In her conversation, there was one phrase repeated often: "at my age... ." There used to be a phrase, "you are as old as you feel." At 93 today, I feel as if I am forty–eight. My feet feel perhaps a little bit older.

Letters congratulating me on my graduation kept arriving. "You are such an inspiration." That embarrassed me, but I am grateful. One friend said, "The connection between cause and effect is often so illusory and disheartening that to see it *really* connected is exhilarating." The *New York Times* even wrote, "Ms. Martindell is charmingly full of the academic enthusiasm normally associated with much younger students."

And it was exhilarating indeed. What a day May 19, 2002, was for all of us. It was so good to have so many of my nearest and dearest relatives there, as well as the daughter of my roommate that freshman year at Smith so many years ago. Mary Rogers Savage, my first college roommate, died a year earlier, but her daughter, Elizabeth was there to celebrate with me.

It had been four years of intensive work, and the last year had been especially difficult. I could do nothing but study, read, and write. I did learn to hone the skills of concentration and analytical thinking, and to remember what I had read. In the words of another returning student, I learned to "find out what I did not know" and to "put education in the context of my experience." One of the reasons for returning was the loss of my dear Toss. I was encouraged by his interest in my education before he died.

I knew it would not be easy to earn a degree, but now I

had the perspective of having lived a full and interesting life, and appreciated what was spread before me.

Unfortunately, there was not sufficient time for all the courses I wanted to take. At graduation, my favorite professor and advisor, Dan Horowitz, toasted me at the Trustee's dinner with a promise. He said he would write a letter to any graduate school if asked, and it would attest that no school should hold it against me that it took almost 70 years to finish my bachelor's degree.

Graduation ceremonies lasted all weekend. May 18 was Ivy Day, when alumnae held reunions and the graduating class paraded, dressed as directed in "white skirts and black shoes." Each one carried a red rose. I went to ask for mine. "What do you want it for, your granddaughter?" I was asked. I proudly declared it was for me.

We lunched, thirty–five family members and some faculty friends, at the Green Street Cafe. My nephew Tim Clark, read an ode in my honor.

Anne Clark Martindell: Nine Decades in Verse

I. Beginnings

In 1914, the year World War One
Was sparked by the tragic assassination
Of King Ferdinand in Sarajevo
And warfare declared by Montenegro,

In that year, when Nixon first saw the light,
And Burroughs first wrote of Tarzan's great might,
A bright star shone over Fifth Avenue,
And stage left Anne entered, too good to be true.

Charlie Chaplin was starring in "Making a Living,"

While Marjorie Blair Clark was busy a'giving
Birth to her child, the first–born of three,
At the Plaza Hotel, in grand luxury.

Sweet Anne was followed by Bill and then Blair,
And, of course, girls were supposed to be silent and fair;
Not much book learning was needed, just manners and such,
Perhaps music and sewing with a feminine touch.
So way back in the 20s, when Aunt Anne was a lass,
Few would think that she'd be at the head of her class,
In politics, government, foreign affairs
And then higher ed, as if on a dare…

To sample each field of human endeavor,
To prove that she's every iota as clever
As any male creature that e'er strode the earth,
She was bound and determined to prove her true worth.

II. Education, Marriage, Children

Way back in the 30s, when the old Model T
Was as new and as modern as any could be,
Aunt Anne from St. Tim's was finally set free
And she set off for Smith for a college degree.

But in the depression when afflicting the land,
It wasn't the sheepskin but rather the hand
Of the eligible young man that counted for most;
For that the Old Man would sure lift a toast.

"We'll make you a debutante," Papa thus decreed,
"All the eligible bachelors to our party will speed,
Eddie Duchin will play at the St. Regis Hotel,
And your charms some nice bachelor surely will fell."

And so came to pass that mean old Papa
Would say to his daughter, "You've come oh so far,
Far enough, I would judge, in fair academe
Now that from yon Richmond arrivest the cream

Of Southern society, the great Baron Scott,
If you don't take his hand you surely will rot,
With the worms and the grubs that lie in the graves
Of unmarried ladies, of dreaded old maids."
Over child–bearing years, quite lightly we'll trip
Without meaning, O muse, entirely to skip,
Th'arrival; of Marjory, David and George,
Roger when Martindell union was forged.

III. The Professional Years

Now Aunt Anne might well say, of the passage of youth,
That not until fifty does one know enough truth,
To see there is more than society teas,
From soirées and matrons one gladly could flee....

And so she'd campaign against faraway war,
In the service of Gene, she'd do her first tour
In the landscape of politics, where she'd engage
Her calling, her passion, her judgment so sage.

Way back in the 20s, who'd have ever guessed
That Aunt Anne in her sixties, Repubs would she best,
Trouncing conservatives, proudly she'd say,
In State Senate, let's go the Democrat way.

Then sweet Jimmy, the farmer from the Plains, came to town,
Singing songs of the South, saying "Please come on down,

And in mah Department of State play a role,
Giving cash where disasters have taken their toll."

Aunt Anne was so good at handing out dough
That old Jimmy said "Ma'am, you just gotta go
To run your own embassy in some foreign land,
Only that will suit a lady so grand."

So off to New Zealand our dear Aunt debarked
And in the land of the sheep she soon made her mark:
Making peace, and not war, out in the Pacific,
As ambassador she was simply terrific.

As a footnote, the bard must not fail to note
That romance in New Zealand suddenly smote
Aunt Anne, young at heart, as plainly one sees,
And artist Toss Woollaston; Ah the birds and the bees!

Public service completed? What next is in store?
For Aunt Anne, she's not finished, she's ready for more.
To Smith College she'd return, that's surely her fate:
Seven decades later? It's never too late.

Two years ago sheepskin was due any day,
And honorary degree, that too was in play,
And the media was on it like ants on sweet jam,
What a story, what glory for glorious Aunt Anne.

To Aunt Anne, The Times devoted most of a page–
Such a story it was, the heart to engage,
And TV—Katie, Jennings and even Oprah
In her eighties Aunt Anne is a media star!

Now the mems are all written and in agents hands

And John Ledyard is next up for biographer Anne's
Literary endeavors, the 10th decade career;
To our diplomat, politician and author, good cheer!

—delivered June 26, 2006, by Timothy B. Clark

All of the family was very proud that I had received
not only a bachelor's degree but an honorary Bachelor of
Laws. A discussion with the honorary degree candidates
took place on Saturday afternoon at three. The other degree
candidates were Anita Hill, Cynthia Moss (Director of the
Anboseli Elephant Research Project in Kenya), Katha Pollitt
(the American feminist writer and regular columnist for *The
Nation*), and Sima Wali from Afghanistan, who championed
the inclusion of women in government. When queried about
my political life, I said that one should take action as a means
to effect change.

We carried our caps and gowns across the street
to Laura Scales Lawn—named for the long–time Smith
administrator—and there we were "robed." Ironically, it was
Laura Scales who was the "warden" in 1933, and it was to her
that I addressed my letter of resignation from Smith that I
was forced to write by my parents.

Bagpipers started to play, increasing the tears that
started to flow as I remembered my sadness in writing that
letter. Dan was my escort up sets of stairs, up the aisles of
cheering students, up to the platform. My seat was directly
behind Lani Guinier, now a law professor at Harvard and the
commencement speaker. Her advice to the students was not to
be afraid to fail. I couldn't have agreed more.

When the bachelor's degree awards were made and I
joined the Adas to march up to receive it, I exclaimed, "At
last!" As I was wired for sound, my exclamation reverberated

and people laughed, applauded, and cried.

After the ceremony, we returned to the president's house. The entire three days had been filmed by NBC's *The Today Show*. They had also come to Princeton to interview me. Bob Dotson, the NBC broadcaster, asked if my father liked women, probing into our relationship. "He liked them horizontal," I said. Bob Dotson grew rosy with embarrassment. That snippet was edited out.

After I got home from graduation, I heard from Smith that Oprah wanted me on her program and was willing to fly me out to Chicago for that purpose. I took my granddaughter Anne, who like me, was a great fan of Oprah's television and her magazine. When we arrived at the studio, one of Oprah's assistants said that Oprah had been in Princeton the day before, where she was awarded an honorary degree. Oprah was so happy about that, she wore her Princeton cap on the plane back to Chicago.

Also on the Oprah show was an 18–year–old young woman who had received a substantial scholarship from Smith to attend in the fall. Her mother had died when she was twelve, leaving her father so distraught that she had to run the family's household. Wanting to help young women, Oprah generously supplemented the Smith scholarship with additional funding for her educational and living expenses. It is this generosity of spirit and graciousness that have made Oprah such a phenomenal success. I was proud to be her guest.

Epilogue

It's been several years now since my graduation from Smith College, and I've come to see quite clearly the value of understanding the lessons of my own history.

How we perform as world citizens, how we are perceived abroad, how we act in concert with other countries —the lessons I learned by being an ambassador—are lessons difficult for some to grasp. President George W. Bush's decision to launch a preemptive war on Iraq, for "reasons" that have since proven erroneous, has earned us the hatred of much of the Muslim world and the skepticism and contempt of many in Europe and even in our own nation. We have lost so many dedicated members of our diplomatic corps who refused to implement Washington's foreign policy. I don't have to be an ambassador to know that anti–American sentiment around the world has never been more pronounced, our motives more in question. With war complicated by fresh and fierce "insurgencies" each week, with casualties mounting, with no end in sight, we need the allies we've alienated.

What encourages me within this picture is the resurgence of positive political activity in our nation and in other nations. Senator Hillary Clinton's impressive record and her tireless dedication to public service has made the possibility of a woman president real. Win or lose, fresh candidates like Barack Obama and John Edwards are capturing voters of every age as they address the issues of stopping the war, providing equal representation to all citizens, closing the gap between the "two Americas"—one consisting of the privileged, the other consisting of the poor and disenfranchised.

A longing for peace is forming in this country, fueled not only by the young who marched in the streets for Martin Luther King Jr. in the late 50s and early 60s, or against the Vietnam war in the 60s, but by citizens of all ages, all walks of life. With the rise of the Internet, information can be disseminated quickly and groups like Common Cause can plan rallies, raise money, gather support for or oppose pieces of legislation with lightening speed.

There are things that I regret, notably that I followed the pattern of my parents' child rearing. One of my children said that he remembered me as a distant figure. All of them have forgiven me, and we are close now, but I did deprive them, as well as myself, of closeness at an important time.

In national terms, what can we do? We seem to be going down a path that our founding fathers would find horrifying, expanding the powers of the President while abandoning the poor on the pretext of promoting an ownership society. Worldwide, as well, we are abandoning the poor. Americans are intrinsically generous but they need to be shown the way. We need to understand that natural resources are limited, that the environment is fragile, and that lesson must be learned before it is too late. If we could all join together, we can see that there is still time for us to act.

The Carter Center, as an example, is committed to advancing human rights and alleviating unnecessary human suffering. Around the world, millions are starving and diseased, and many are right here in our own country.

We have the opportunity, each of us, to be well informed and to seek to understand the complexities of our time and place. We can become students of our own history—personal, political, global—learning its lessons, leaving behind the repetitive cycle of its mistakes, and continually striving for positive change. It's never too late.